Masters of cinema

George Lucas

CAHIERS DU CINEMA

Karina Longworth

Contents

Harrison Ford in *Indiana Jones and the Last Crusade* (1989).

Introduction

George Lucas emerged from the same movement in American filmmaking as Martin Scorsese, Peter Bogdanovich, William Friedkin, and Lucas's close friend and mentor Francis Ford Coppola, but Lucas, the sole native Californian of the bunch, would ultimately take a radically different approach to cinema. His contemporaries, in their intellectual bents and emphases on writing and performance—the aspects of film borrowed from theater—processed the influence of post-war international cinema into character-driven films infused with cynicism and political fatalism. Early in his career, Lucas made a conscious decision to move in the opposite direction. He sought to make films that would stimulate the senses more than the cerebrum, offering old-fashioned escapist pleasures while emphasizing craft and technological innovation.

"How do you personally get to the point where you wake up out of your stupor and take charge of your life and do dangerous and scary things?" This is how Lucas himself summed up the question underlining all of his films, in 2005[1]. Lucas's critics might suggest that when it comes to his own career, that's a question the filmmaker has not been able to answer. Having built an empire in Northern California encompassing production, post-production, and effects facilities, Lucas has the wherewithal to literally do whatever he wants. And yet, for the past two decades, while often proclaiming a desire to make experimental, non-commercial films, he has invested most of his time and fortune into keeping the Star Wars and Indiana Jones franchises humming. But Lucas's self-financed Star Wars prequels—arguably as close to an uncorrupted vision as anything he's ever made—prove that personal filmmaking and franchise maintenance are not necessarily mutually exclusive pursuits. Some might argue that Lucas has simply bought himself the freedom to make films that satisfy only him—the mark of an iconoclast if there ever was one.

Mark Hamill in *The Empire Strikes Back* (1980).

Early life

From *Look at Life* to *Electronic Labyrinth THX 1138 4EB*

"I don't make a work of art; I make a movie."
George Lucas

George Lucas directing the
documentary *Filmmaker* (1968).

Birth of a passion

Born in 1944 in the sleepy Northern California town of Modesto, George Lucas is often credited as a leading light of the first generation of American filmmakers to grow up watching television, only to carry inevitably its influence into cinema. But the Lucas family, who lived on a walnut ranch outside town, didn't actually own a TV set until the mid-1950s. In fact, radio dramas (of which Orson Welles' *The War of the Worlds*, broadcast in 1938, is a famous example) were Lucas's earliest, and perhaps most formative, form of entertainment. By his own admission, he didn't care much for movies until college. "When I went to the movies [as a teenager], I really didn't pay much attention," Lucas remembers. "I was usually going to look for girls or goof off." [2]

Uninterested in school, Lucas was a poor student. As a teenager he devoted the bulk of his attention to Modesto's drag-racing subculture. The young Lucas focused his free time on learning how to fix, build, and race custom cars, eventually immortalizing his experiences in *American Graffiti*. In fact, Lucas may never have made a film at all had his passion for cars not nearly been the death of him. At age seventeen, Lucas was involved in a near-fatal car crash that would change his priorities, and his fate.

Taking mercy on him, Lucas's high school waived required work that he had yet to complete, and let him graduate despite a failing grade point average. Lucas emerged scared away from his dream of a career in car racing, and enrolled in Modesto Junior College in 1963 with the vague notion of pursuing another hobby, painting.

It was around this time that Lucas started spending time in San Francisco, hanging out in jazz clubs and cafés, where he was exposed to, and avidly embraced, experimental film. Lucas first saw the avant-garde, non-narrative shorts of Stan Brakhage, Jordan Belson, and Bruce Conner thanks to Bruce Baillie's Canyon Cinema screenings, a filmmakers' cooperative specializing in the distribution of avant-garde films. These painterly films, most of them made by a single person outside of and indifferent to the Hollywood system, appealed to Lucas both as a loner and rebel and as a visualist.

Lucas longed to transfer from junior college to one of the major film schools in Los Angeles— the University of California at Los Angeles (UCLA) or the University of Southern California (USC)—but both colleges rejected him. On a trip to LA to look for work, Lucas met future cinematographer Haskell Wexler at a racetrack. Wexler, who at that point

Cosmic cinema

"[My] films are not meant to be explained, analyzed, or understood. They are more experiential, more like listening to music." Those words could have come from the mouth of George Lucas, but in fact, the quote is attributed to Jordan Belson, whose short, non-narrative, often cosmological film experiments were a major influence on Lucas, not least in his visual approach to *Star Wars*. Born in 1926 in Chicago, Belson trained as a painter at the University of California at Berkeley. Inspired by the "Art in Cinema" screenings of avant-garde works at the San Francisco Museum of Modern Art, Belson began making animated films using his paintings as raw material. Rather than painting on a strip of 35mm film, he would create a series of paintings on a scroll, and photograph each image for several frames, to create the illusion of motion. A major part of the 1950s Beat scene in San Francisco, Belson painted the mural on the facade of the City Lights Bookstore. In 1953, Belson made what film historian William Moritz called the "great masterpiece of [his] early films," *Mandala*. With its pulsing geometric shapes and Gamelan score, *Mandala* aimed to serve as a meditative object,

and it was the first of many Belson films to tie in to Eastern spiritualism. After collaborating in the late 1950s with electronic music composer Henry Jacobs on a series of experimental, non-narrative film and music presentations at the San Francisco Planetarium, called the Vortex Concerts, Belson began work on what are thought of as his nine "mature" works, beginning with *Re-Entry* in 1964. That title was meant to reference both Belson's return to filmmaking after a hiatus and the "re-entry" of astronaut John Glenn, snippets of whose radio communications are heard on the soundtrack. Indeed, space travel was on Belson's mind: films like *Cycles* (1975) and *Light* (1973) are kaleidoscopic explorations of light and shapes that distinctly evoke galactic space, while functioning as mystical objects. Belson's abstract, psychedelic, spiritual films, some of them comprised of galaxy-like imagery, offer an important frame of reference in terms of understanding how Lucas's love of experimental film directly influenced some of the biggest blockbusters of all time: the Star Wars series. The pulsing vortexes of light on a backdrop of infinite black space in Belson's *Allures*

(1961) bear a clear resemblance to the images of outer space as a highway and as a battlefield seen in *Star Wars*. Belson's facility for creating seductive, fantastic imagery attracted the attention of commercial filmmakers. Donald Cammel incorporated bits of imagery shot by Belson in his 1977 sci-fi film *Demon Seed*, and Belson was later invited to create cosmic special effects for Philip Kaufman's space program film, *The Right Stuff* (1983), which included a dramatization of Glenn's orbit of the Earth.

For some years, an aura of mystery surrounded Belson's work. He was reticent to reveal his methods ("His studio is like a monastery for film creation," Kaufman said.), and reluctant to have his work exhibited under non-ideal circumstances. But in later years he worked with the Center for Visual Music on exhibitions of his films, and in 2007, he curated a DVD containing five pieces, with the stipulation that the buyer agreed not to publicly screen the films or disseminate them online. He died of heart failure in 2011.

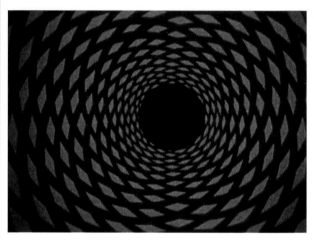

Allures by Jordan Belson (1961).

had just served as director of photography on Elia Kazan's *America, America* (1963), would become the first in a series of professional mentors whose connections and experience Lucas would absorb, and eventually surpass. Lucas built a stock car for Wexler; Wexler helped the academically unremarkable Lucas get into USC's film school.

David versus Goliath

Lucas entered USC in 1964. At that time, film school—even the top film schools in Los Angeles, of which USC was one—was not considered a sure path to Hollywood success. With union regulations designed to keep outsiders from taking even the most menial jobs, the film industry was then a walled garden, most readily accessible by nepotism. But all of that was about to change, thanks to the

New Hollywood wave kicked off by the successes of films like Arthur Penn's *Bonnie and Clyde* (1967) and Dennis Hopper's *Easy Rider* (1969), and which was characterized by a rise in power of film directors.

At USC, Lucas met many of those with whom he'd work for decades to come. They included the cinematographer-to-be Caleb Deschanel (Philip Kaufman's *The Right Stuff*, 1983); John Milius (*Conan the Barbarian*, 1982; co-writer of Francis Ford Coppola's *Apocalypse Now*, 1979); Matthew Robbins (writer of Steven Spielberg's *Sugarland Express*, 1974); Walter Murch, who would become a pioneering sound designer and editor; and Willard Huyck, the screenwriter who, with his wife Gloria Katz, would collaborate with Lucas on *American Graffiti*, *Indiana Jones and the Temple of Doom* (1984), and *Howard the Duck* (1986). Lucas and friends were united by an "us vs them" vibe.

It seemed impossible to break into Hollywood, so they banded together to help one another realize personal projects. They were the first generation of American film students to be influenced more by world cinema than by the Hollywood canon. Turned on to the French New Wave and Fellini by Murch, and to Japanese master Akira Kurosawa by Milius, Lucas devoured films like Kurosawa's *The Hidden Fortress* (1958) and *Seven Samurai* (1954)—both of which would heavily influence the Star Wars series.

Lucas also expanded his taste for experimental film. He would later say he staged the first *Star Wars* film with the documentaries of Claude Jutra (a sometime collaborator of Francois Truffaut and Jean Rouch) in mind, blocking dialogue scenes loosely in front of multiple cameras in the hopes of injecting some spontaneity into the performances of his anything-but-naturalistic dialogue (*À tout prendre*, 1963). He was even more influenced by Arthur Lipsett, a documentary editor who made avant-garde collage films on the side (*Very Nice, Very Nice*, 1961). Lucas, whose talent for editing was already apparent (he had immediately responded to the upright Moviola's resemblance to a car, with its pedals and hand brake), decided to model his career after Lipsett's. Lipsett's de-tethering of sound and image would profoundly influence Lucas's work with sound editor Murch on his first feature, *THX 1138* (1971). Lucas would repay the influence by inserting subliminal references to Lipsett's short *21-87* into several of his films: *THX* is set in the year 2187, and in *Star Wars Episode IV: A New Hope* (1977), Leia is imprisoned in cell 21-87.

California of the mid-'60s was a hotbed of anti-establishment and youth-culture activity. While Lucas himself wasn't a hippie (in fact, he'd later categorize *American Graffiti* as an attempt to capture the last moment of genuine innocence before

George Lucas filming his student short, *6-18-67* (1967), on the set of *Mackenna's Gold*.

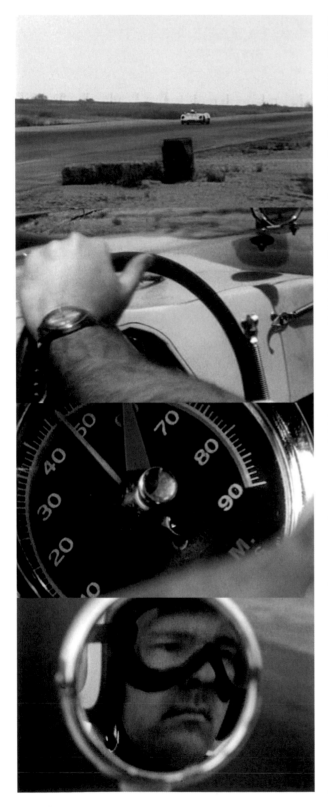

Peter Brock in *1:42:08 A Man and His Car* (1966).

drug-fueled anger took over youth culture), he and his USC cronies saw their pursuit of filmmaking as a challenge to the dominant order. While their peers were fearlessly staring down political authority through protesting the Vietnam War, Lucas and friends saw themselves as Davids fighting against the Goliath of Hollywood. "We never thought we were going to make money at it, or that it was a good way to become famous," Lucas would later say of his college gang. "It was like an addiction."[3]

The first shorts

Lucas pursued his "addiction" to the hilt. His first student film, *Look at Life* (1965), is a one-minute short produced for an animation class, montaging iconic youth-culture photographs of the early '60s. Lucas made nine films in three years, using his own money to pay for extra film stock above the allotment given by USC to every student.

While still a student, Lucas was hired as a cameraman for Saul Bass, the great poster and title designer, and shot drag-racing footage for the titles of John Frankenheimer's *Grand Prix* (1966). It was on the set of *Grand Prix* that Lucas met racing driver Peter Brock, and convinced him to loan his time and his car for the production of *1:42.08: A Man and His Car* (1966), a short portrait of Peter Brock test driving his Lotus 23 car on a deserted stretch of California highway. This film fascinates for its embryonic suggestions of Lucas' unique cinematic style. Shot with gliding and zooming cameras both inside and outside the vehicle, edited so that the perspective is constantly swapping between the driver and an invisible spectator, its fetishistic treatment of a fast vehicle and the vast possibility of the desert point directly to key aesthetic tropes of the Star Wars films. Perhaps more significantly, *1:42.08* shows Lucas taking as his subject not a man, an action, or an object, but a sensation: it's a movie in which every creative decision is made in orde&r to communicate to the viewer what it feels like to drive too fast. It's an early pointer to what may be Lucas's most valuable talent: the ability to put a viewer inside an adventure. Lucas exited USC in 1966 proficient in shooting, producing, directing, and editing; as classmate Robert Dalva (who directed *Star Wars: Attack of the Clones* in 2010) said later, "The modus operandi of USC was not to teach you a craft, but to teach you all the crafts."[4]

Arthur Lipsett: origins of the Force

George Lucas has proven to be nothing if not susceptible to influence—he even likened *Star Wars* to "a very big sundae" of "all the things that are great put together"—but few of those influences have been referenced in Lucas's films as frequently as avant-garde filmmaker Arthur Lipsett.

Lipsett began his career as an animator and sound collagist employed by the National Film Board of Canada. He was nominated for an Oscar in 1962 for his seven-minute short, *Very Nice, Very Nice* (1961), a montage of still images set to a soundscape compiled from bits of discarded audio Lipsett found in the trash at work. Lipsett didn't win the Oscar, but the film did attract the attention of Stanley Kubrick, who reportedly asked Lipsett to edit the trailer for *Dr. Strangelove*—an offer Lipsett turned down. The influence of *Very Nice, Very Nice* can be seen in Lucas's very first completed film, the still-image collage *Look at Life*, made in 1965. Lipsett's next film, *21-87* (1964), was a more radical found image and sound collage, using unrelated images and sounds (factory noises laid over footage of an autopsy, apparently carefree teenagers soundtracked with labored breathing) to create a bleak essay on the state of human existence. For Lucas, the film was a revelation, and he expressed his debt to Lipsett in more ways than one. Structurally, *21-87* was a major reference for Lucas's first feature, *THX 1138* (1971). As his collaborator Walter Murch would remember later, "When George saw *21-87*, a lightbulb went off. One of the things we clearly wanted to do in *THX* was to make a film where the sound and the pictures were free-floating." The most substantial connection between Lipsett's work and Lucas's comes from an audio snatch in *21-87* of a conversation between Warren S. McCulloch and Roman Kroitor, the former an artificial intelligence specialist, the latter a cinematographer and IMAX developer (a motion picture film format that enables the display of very large, very high-resolution images) about the mystery of human life. Kroiter says, "Many people feel that in the contemplation of nature and in communication with other living things, they become aware of some kind of force, or something, behind this apparent mask which we see in front of us, and they call it God." Lucas later acknowledged that this quote was the inspiration for The Force, the mysterious power at the center of the Star Wars mythology.

Lucas and Lipsett never met. The Canadian filmmaker suffered from severe bipolar disorder, and he completed just three personal films before committing suicide in 1986.

21-87 by Arthur Lipsett (1964).

Lucas prepared to be drafted, but the US Army declared him unfit because he suffered from diabetes. He got a job as an assistant editor at the United States Information Agency, where he worked under Verna Fields (later the editor of *American Graffiti*) and alongside fellow editor Marcia Griffin, whom he married in 1969. Disillusioned with creating propaganda films for the US government, Lucas soon decided to return to USC for graduate studies.

In June 1967 his connection to Saul Bass helped him land a place on a project Bass was supervising: Lucas and three other students were given access to the set of J. Lee Thompson's *Mackenna's Gold* (1969), a Columbia Pictures Western starring Gregory Peck and Omar Sharif, and were assigned to make films about the production. While his classmates made typical behind-the-scenes documentaries, Lucas, stunned by the excess of the bloated studio film, went off alone and made a poetic, nonnarrative portrait of the isolation and beauty of the film's desert locale, *6-18-67* (1967). But Lucas's major project in graduate school was *Electronic Labyrinth THX 1138 4EB* (1967)—his most well-known short, his first experiment in science fiction, and the template for his first feature film.

Meeting Coppola

Perhaps the single most definitive aspect of Lucas's college years was his friendship and business partnership with Francis Ford Coppola. Both men had big

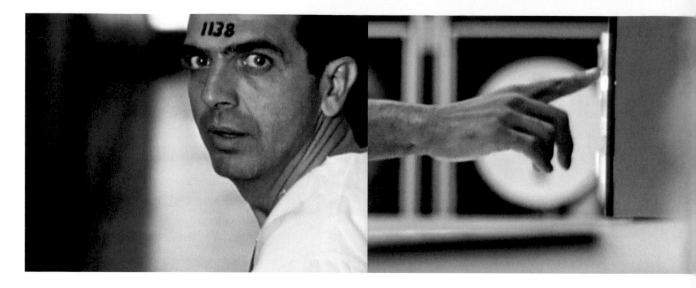

ideas about challenging the way movies were made, both creatively and economically. Their friendship happened due to a highly symbolic accident: they were essentially thrown together thanks to the sorry state of Warner Brothers. In 1968, Lucas was awarded a scholarship that allowed him to pick an internship on the WB lot. He chose the animation department, hoping to study with Chuck Jones and the creators of Bugs Bunny and *Looney Tunes*, but arriving at the studio, he found that the department had been recently shut down. He chose to work instead on the set of the Fred Astaire musical fantasy *Finian's Rainbow* (1968), which Coppola was directing.

Coppola and Lucas had a few things in common, including a film school background (Coppola had graduated from USC's rival, UCLA), which was not typical on movie sets at the time. At only five years apart, they were still kids compared to the dinosaurs roaming around the studio and, while neither was exactly bohemian, both were distinctly not of the establishment. Francis recognized George as "the only other beard on the lot," and promoted him from intern to administrative assistant.[5] *Finian's Rainbow*, a money loser and critical punching bag, was a disappointment from the studio's perspective, but its production would prove to be a landmark for the new Hollywood. Coppola became a role model for the generation of would-be *auteurs* and actors emerging from the film schools and migrating west from New York. To Walter Murch, Coppola was "one of us, a film student without any connections to the film business, [who] had put one

foot in front of another and actually made a feature film sponsored by one of the studios."[6]

Coppola invited Lucas to serve as an all-purpose assistant on his next project, *The Rain People* (1969), a drama about a woman who leaves her family for a few days (the story was inspired by experiences of Coppola's mother). Coppola put his own money into *The Rain People* to "prime the pump" for studio investment, a move that earned Lucas's respect. Coppola's plan was to travel across the country, starting in New York and moving west, shooting the movie along the way and editing dailies in mobile homes on the road. Coppola arranged a job for Lucas, shooting a behind-the-scenes documentary of the production. That documentary, titled simply *Filmmaker* (1968), is a much more traditional backstage portrait than the short Lucas made on the set of *Mackenna's Gold*: this was a production Lucas didn't need to subvert through documentation, because its very reason for being was to constitute a cheaper, more personal alternative to the Hollywood assembly line.

The job was in some sense just an excuse to get Lucas on the payroll so he could collect checks while writing the feature version of *THX*, which Coppola planned to produce. Drunk on what they were getting away with on the open road, Coppola and Lucas started plotting their independence.

Above: Dan Natchsheim in *Electronic Labyrinth THX 1138 4EB* (1967).

Opposite page: George Lucas with Francis Ford Coppola on the set of *THX 1138* (1971).

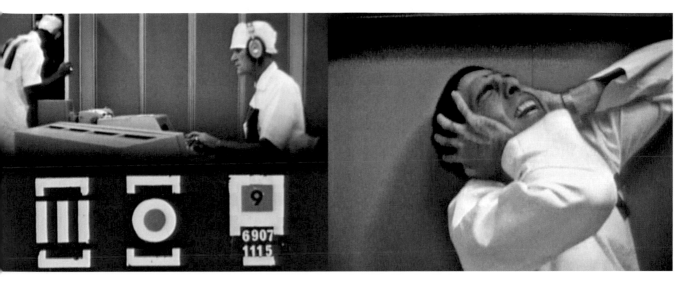

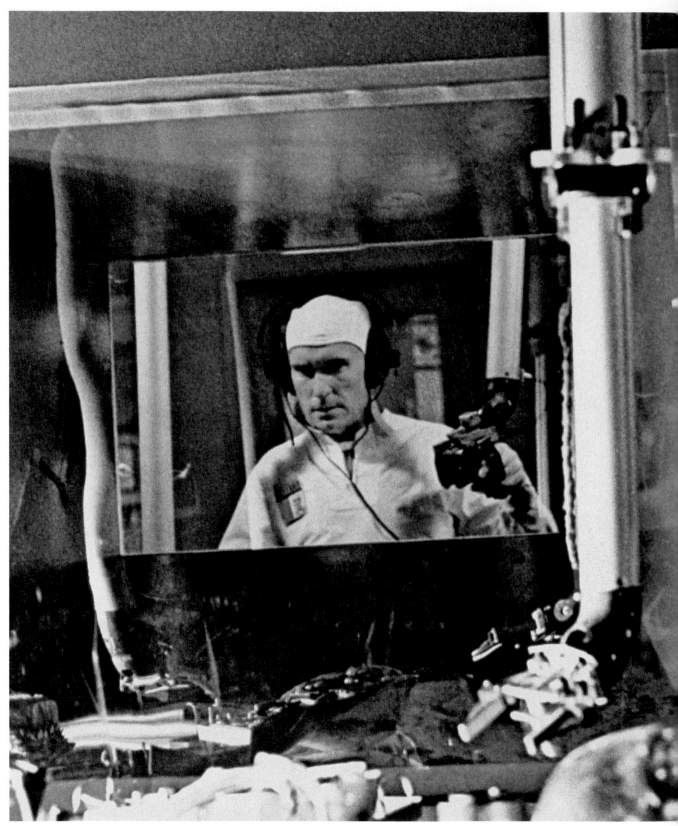

The Coppola years

Robert Duvall
in *THX 1138* (1971).

American Zoetrope

In Hollywood in the late 1960s, Francis Ford Coppola was a little fish in a large pond. In 1969, galvanized in part by the success of the independently produced *Easy Rider* and in part by his own experience making *The Rain People* far from the prying eyes of a studio, Coppola made a move to create his own pond.

American Zoetrope was conceived by its founders—Coppola and Lucas, plus members of the USC crew, including Caleb Deschanel and Walter Murch—as a full-service production and post-production company, a Hollywood away from Hollywood, where artists, not businessmen, would make the rules. "What we're striving for is total freedom," Lucas said in 1971, "where we can finance our pictures, make them our way, release them where we want them released and be completely free to express ourselves. That's very hard to do in the world of business. In this country, the only thing that speaks is money and you have to have the money in order to have the power to be free." "We don't want to make their kind of movies," Lucas concluded simply. "We want to do something completely different."[7] San Francisco was chosen as the home for the utopian experiment. That Lucas had roots in nearby Modesto had less to do with the choice of location than the simple fact that the Northern California city was far enough from Hollywood to represent a break, yet accessible to Los Angeles—still the home of the industry's money and power—via a one-hour flight.

Since Coppola was not yet personally solvent enough to set up Zoetrope without Hollywood money, he planned to attract an investment of studio funds to get Zoetrope's first few films off the ground, and then use profits from those films to finance future projects. He sold Warner Brothers' John Calley on a slate of films in various stages of development, including what would become *The Conversation* (1974) and *Apocalypse Now* (1979), and Lucas's feature-length expansion of his student short, *THX 1138*—the first planned Zoetrope production. Calley would invest a total of $600,000 in Zoetrope, and in return, Warner Brothers would own the rights to each of the films in Coppola's package.

In the fall of 1969, Coppola took a lease on two floors of warehouse space at 827 Folsom and got to work cutting *The Rain People* on brand-new, European-imported editing tables. Coppola spared no expense setting up the office, which from the start irked spendthrift Lucas, who was named vice-president of the company. Still, as much as the intention was to foster an anything-goes climate of creative freedom in no small part inspired by what Dennis Hopper and crew were able to pull off with *Easy Rider*, the Zoetrope gang was different in one key respect: it was a drug-free workplace. They may have been rebels, but they were also squares.

Disillusionment

Coppola tried to convince his young protégé that if he wanted to make movies, he had to learn how to put what was in his head into screenplay form, not least as a process of learning how to communicate with actors. But Lucas knew his first draft of the *THX* screenplay was terrible. With the help of Walter Murch, Lucas was able to produce a viable rewrite, but *THX* was always meant to be light on story and dialogue and heavy on design and visual metaphor. Filming began in September 1969 in San Francisco. Coppola, as executive producer, stood between Lucas and Warner Brothers, allowing the director to work without interference from the studio.

THX 1138 (1971) stars Robert Duval as THX, the titular citizen of a future underground totalitarian state. Citizens are under constant surveillance and drugged into passively accepting controls like mandated headshaving and the criminalization of romance. THX's roommate, LUH (Maggie McOmie), stops taking her state-ordered tranquilizers and tinkers with THX's allotment of pills in order to awaken his long-dormant sex drive. The pair fall in love, or something like it, but they can't evade the eyes of the state and are soon imprisoned. THX manages to escape and goes on the run. He's pursued by the police, who give chase until they burn through their allotted budget.

In search of a near-documentary look, Lucas ordered that his actors shave their heads and wear no make-up, and he kept lighting minimal. He did few rehearsals and no blocking. "There were no marks and no measurements," he said. "The cameramen just had to guess where the actors were, while riding focus blind in a lot of cases."[8] Only one set was built for the film. The production managed

Robert Duvall
in *THX 1138* (1971).

THX 1138 (1971).

Following pages: Maggie McOmie and Robert Duvall in *THX 1138* (1971).

to save loads of money by judiciously selecting real locations in and around San Francisco, including the half-finished Bay Area Rapid Transit subway system. The use of present-day California as a double for *THX*'s future dystopia made more than just economic sense: for Lucas, the film was really about the world he lived in. The human condition circa 1970, particularly in Hollywood, was, as he saw it, crippled and blinded by fear. Lucas described his colleagues as "people in cages with open doors."[9] In *THX*, the enforcement of the foundational ideals and standards of the system—quality control, in essence—is forced to take a backseat to cost control. It was a not-so-veiled attack on the film industry. "Everyone else calls it science fiction. I call it documentary fantasy," Lucas said. "The film is the way I see LA right now ... the idea that we are all living in cages and the doors are wide open, and all we have to do is walk out."[10]

Lucas edited the picture himself, during the day, while Walter Murch edited sound at night. The interplay between sound and image would bear strongly the influence of the experimental non-fiction films Lucas binged on at USC. With most

characters speaking in a drugged-out monotone, Murch's multi-layered audio collage soundtrack crucially fleshes out the film's emotional tonality. There's a strong ironic tension: the standards of the state are enforced via artificially optimistic platitudes and euphemisms, which ring false with the bland, lifeless society seen on screen.

Though Warner Brothers had financed the film and was under contract to release it, the studio had no involvement in the production, thanks to Coppola's protection of his protégé, and didn't see a frame of film until Lucas was finished with his edit. Lucas had proven the efficiency of the independent approach—THX came in under its $750,000 budget and was in the can inside the ten-week shooting schedule. But that mattered little, since Warners hated the movie. They had gone into business with Zoetrope expecting to get low-budget flicks that could be marketed easily into youth-friendly hits—just like Easy Rider. THX, a painfully cynical, yet dryly funny, manifesto on freedom, was not what the studio had in mind. Coppola had been telling both Lucas and Warner Brothers what they wanted to hear, which meant he was being disingenuous to

both. After a disastrous test screening for WB executives, Coppola pretended he was unprepared for the experimental feature that was shown. "I don't know what the fuck this is," he assured Warners.[11] Worried that the studio would seize the film right then and there, a crew of Lucas's friends successfully smuggled the work print out of the screening room. WB nonetheless managed to assign "youth expert" Fred Weintraub to recut THX. He ended up shaving a total of four minutes. Lucas was livid, not only because he felt it was a violation of his vision, but also because he felt the cuts were arbitrary, meant to show him who was boss and not to make the movie more commercial. Lucas saw the release version for the first time on opening day with a paying audience.

THX was a huge flop, and even those close to Lucas had difficulty supporting it. "It left me cold," admitted Marcia Lucas.[12] After the failure of THX, Warners backed out of their deal with Coppola to support Zoetrope. This was the beginning of straight-laced, control-freak Lucas's disillusionment with his mentor. Coppola was a supportive father figure to Lucas, who had a strained relationship with his conservative—businessman biological

From American Zoetrope to Skywalker Ranch

American Zoetrope was envisioned as the locus of a Stateside new wave in the model of the European cinema new waves. The idea was sparked on the 1968 set of *The Rain People.* Director Francis Ford Coppola realized that if he didn't need a studio's facilities in order to make a movie, he could do it anywhere—"It didn't need to be in Hollywood." A trip Coppola took to Europe in 1968 added fuel to the fire. He was particularly impressed by his visit to Laterna, a Danish filmmaking collective housed in a seaside mansion. Laterna made commercials, soft-core porn, and feature films. The members lived and worked together. The house was full of editing rooms, and the grounds were full of gorgeous young Danish women. Laterna's figurehead, Mogens Skot-Hansen, collected antique movie equipment. He gave Coppola a zoetrope as a parting gift. When Coppola

returned to the United States, he breathlessly recounted the wonders of Laterna to Lucas, who was all for making movies outside of Hollywood—both the geographical location and the state of mind. Together with Caleb Deschanel, Walter Murch, and other young up-and-comers trained in Los Angeles but more inspired by European art house cinema, Coppola and Lucas envisioned Zoetrope as a full-service mini-studio, where they could help one another create personal films without having to bend to the demands of the studio system.

When it came time to set up American Zoetrope's offices, Coppola was insistent on finding space in the city of San Francisco rather than its more pastoral outskirts, which Lucas would have preferred—he thought removing themselves from the distractions of the city was part of the point

of the experiment. Soon, Lucas became further disillusioned with Coppola's profligate spending and *laissez-faire* attitude toward management. Lucas had seen Zoetrope as a retreat from the pressures and influence of Hollywood, a place to make films truly independently. But Zoetrope was funded by a studio—Warner Brothers—and entirely dependent on making that studio happy. They were not happy with Lucas's *THX*, the first feature to be completed under the auspices of Zoetrope, and in November 1970, WB demanded repayment of its investment. While Coppola would hold on to the Zoetrope brand, and still produces films under the label today, the would-be independent collective did not survive the traumatic *THX* experience.

But Lucas didn't give up on the dream of filmmaking as a retreat. He was able to replicate the Laterna vibe, to some

extent, during post-production on *American Graffiti*, when Coppola bought a house along the river in Mill Valley and set up editing studios in the coach house. And then, in 1978, as *The Empire Strikes Back* was in pre-production, George and Marcia Lucas bought Bulltail Ranch. They renamed it Skywalker Ranch, and Lucas at first claimed it would serve as a "think tank" for filmmakers. But it was not the bohemian aspects of Laterna that Lucas was interested in replicating. Instead, he took the notion of "retreat" more literally: he wanted to create all of the facilities of a full-service studio right in his backyard, so that he could beat a permanent retreat from Hollywood.

Geroge Lucas (standing on the truck) and the crew of Francis Ford Coppola's *The Rain People* (1969).

father. Coppola was always building his ego, telling Lucas he was a genius—but Lucas was too used to rebelling against father figures to fall comfortably into Coppola's image. "My life is kind of a reaction against Francis' life," he said later. "I'm his antithesis." [13] Both Coppola and Marcia suggested that he had better follow up the "cold" *THX* with something more emotional. As Lucas put it in 1980, "I thought, 'You want warm and human? I'll give you warm and human.'" [14]

Nostalgic escapism

Set on the last night of summer in a small, Northern California town in 1962, *American Graffiti* (1973) tells the story of four teenage friends vacillating between childhood and adulthood. Curt (Richard Dreyfuss) has a scholarship to an East Coast university but, the night before he's scheduled to get on a cross-country plane, he's having doubts about leaving his hometown behind. He's supposed to make the trip with Steve (Ron Howard), who is dating Curt's younger sister Laurie (Cindy Williams), although Steve has suggested that each of them "see other people" while he's away at school. While Steve, Laurie, and Curt head off to the local sock hop, their friends Terry the Toad and John Millner cruise the town's main drag. The film tracks each young man's adventures from

American Graffiti (1973).

sundown to sun up—the girls they meet, flirt, and bicker with; the obstacles they face in the form of authority figures and older, cooler dudes; the pressing decisions bounded up in the larger question of what kind of men they're going to turn out to be. In what was a groundbreaking storytelling tactic for a fictional film at the time, Lucas interweaves each character's story, cutting back and forth until their paths intersect at a climactic drag race.

Lucas envisioned *American Graffiti* as both an American version of Fellini's *I Vitteloni* (1953)—a comedy-drama about a group of young people hanging out and contemplating the future, the last days of summer functioning as a metaphor for the end of adolescence—and a kind of fantasy version of his own high-school autobiography, with so much period pop music commenting on and helping to tell the story that it would almost function as a musical. The characters don't sing and rarely dance, but *American Graffiti* does recall a mid-century Hollywood musical in its vibrant color palette and narrative that weaves musical set pieces together with character-based scenes. As a one-night-in-the-city movie interweaving the stories of a group of male friends in common but separate search of adventure before sunrise, it's

not dissimilar to Stanley Donen and Gene Kelly's *On the Town* (1949).

THX had been a highly metaphoric take on what Lucas saw as the hypocrisy and homogeneity of contemporary Hollywood. It was an experiment in personal filmmaking that had failed commercially. For his follow-up, Lucas knew he needed to take a different approach, telling a personal story. "I realized after making *THX* that those problems were so real that most of us have to face those things every day, so we're in a constant state of frustration," Lucas said. "That just makes us more depressed than we were before. So [with *American Graffiti*], I made a film where, essentially, we can get rid of some of those frustrations, the feeling that everything seems futile." Lucas also was nostalgic for his own, comparatively innocent teen years spent tooling around with cars and cruising the main drag of Modesto. "It was the mating ritual of my times, before it disappeared and everybody got into psychedelia and drugs," he said. [15]

As much as *American Graffiti* is unquestionably, and intentionally, a work of nostalgic escapism, like *THX* it can be read as a self-portrait of Lucas's struggles to assert himself as a filmmaker in a suffocating, essentially provincial climate. At that time, Lucas was becoming disillusioned with Zoetrope, and with Coppola in particular, but he was reluctant to give up the dream and submit to powerlessness in Hollywood. Like Curt, Lucas had to choose between the easy, safe option of sticking with the pack, or else forge ahead alone and face the unknown, risking failure in the name of greater potential reward. Like his protagonist, Lucas chose the latter. In plumbing memories of a

Above: Paul Le Mat, Cindy Williams and Ron Howard in *American Graffiti* (1973).

Opposite page: Mackenzie Phillips and Paul Le Mat in *American Graffiti* (1973).

Paul Le Mat
in *American Graffiti* (1973).

Happy Days

Premiering on American television in January 1974, the family sitcom *Happy Days*—about high school kid Richie Cunningham, played by Ron Howard, and his social life, which revolved around a small-town drive-in diner—bore such a strong resemblance to *American Graffiti*, which had been a blockbuster at the US box office the previous summer, that some presumed the TV show had been spun off from the movie. In fact, the seed of *Happy Days* long preceded George Lucas's movie.

In 1971, Howard was cast—alongside Harold Gould, Marion Ross, and Anson Williams—in a television pilot called *New Family in Town*. The pilot was not picked up for a weekly series, but instead was retitled *Love and the Happy Days*, and presented as part of the television anthology series, *Love American Style*, in February 1972. Lucas saw the pilot, and subsequently cast Howard in *American Graffiti*, which began shooting in June 1972. When the movie became a huge hit, the television network ABC, in hopes of capitalizing on the wave of 1950s nostalgia inspired by *American Graffiti*, partially recast (Tom Bosley replaced Harold Gould as the patriarch of the Cunningham family), and reshot the original pilot as *Happy Days*. *Happy Days* wasn't a hit initially, but by its fourth season it had become the most watched show on American television, and new episodes were produced through 1984.

Candy Clark and Charles Martin Smith in *American Graffiti* (1973).

"simpler" time, Lucas was actively launching a counterstrike to the "depressing" films made by his New Hollywood peers.

But giving them "warm and human" was harder than Lucas thought. After United Artists rejected Lucas's first draft of the screenplay, he asked his old friends, screenwriting couple Willard Huyck and Gloria Katz, to help him round out the characters, and then pitched the film to Universal, who were mounting a slate of low-budget "youth" movies. Universal agreed to take it, on one condition: that Francis Ford Coppola, suddenly hot from *The Godfather* (1972), executive produced. Lucas longed to step outside of his mentor's shadow, but that would have to wait. Universal first offered an investment of $600,000, which would have to cover everything—the production budget, salaries, and an enormous amount of music licensing fees. Lucas's agent managed to get the studio to throw in an extra $150,000—but Lucas had to give up his right to final cut in order to get it.

The most profitable American film ever

The bulk of the film was shot in Petaluma, a small town in Northern California's Marin County, where the underfunded production settled in for nearly a month of night shoots. Lucas shot every scene with two cameras, so that the actors never knew when they were "on," and thus would never turn their characters "off." Lucas felt that he didn't have time to make directorial choices on set—he'd have to "direct" in the editing room. Unhappy with the look of the first dailies, Lucas persuaded Haskell Wexler to shoot the movie as a personal favor, for free, at night after days spent shooting commercials in Los Angeles. Wexler got the look Lucas wanted—all lurid neon, like the inside of a jukebox.

Lucas had conceived three of the four main characters as versions of himself. Bespectacled dweeb Terry the Toad, Lucas said, was "how I started: always the littlest guy, never quite able to make it. When I got to be 16 and got a car I started racing ... that would be John. Then I had that very bad accident and spent time in the hospital. After that I started to apply myself to my studies and became sort of like Curt. I still went down to cruise, to hang out, but I was more detached ... I could reflect on it." [16] But he needed the Huycks to help him write Steve, the ostensibly well-adjusted college-bound kid played by Ron Howard, who spends much of the movie cavalierly pushing his girlfriend to have sex.

With some needling from Lucas, Coppola bought a house in Mill Valley and turned the attic into an editing room. Verna Fields—the editor in whose office Lucas and Marcia first met—was brought in to cut the picture, with Lucas's now-wife serving as her assistant. Away from Hollywood, working with hand-selected friends, it looked, for a brief instant, as though American Zoetrope could succeed after all.

At a test screening in San Francisco January 1973, *American Graffiti* got a huge response from the audience, including a standing ovation. But Universal's Ned Tanen assumed Lucas and Coppola had filled their hometown crowd with friends. In its

From *Easy Rider* to *Love Story*

Made for just $400,000, put up by the independent production company BBS, Dennis Hopper's *Easy Rider* grossed $19 million in the summer of 1969. It was nominated for two Oscars, and won the First Film Award at the Cannes Film Festival. This film made outside the Hollywood system had done what Hollywood itself was trying, and failing, to do: turn the new generation of young people, which was driving the culture in so many ways, into moviegoers. The success of *Easy Rider* briefly opened a window in which studios turned to companies like BBS and American Zoetrope as a cost-effective method of obtaining films geared toward young people.

That window essentially closed for good with the December 1970 release of Arthur Hiller's *Love Story*. Like *Easy Rider*, *Love Story* was a movie made for viewers in their teens and twenties; like *Easy Rider*, it was a big hit, grossing over $100 million on a production budget of around $2 million. The similarities end there. *Easy Rider*—a film about drug-addled societal dropouts filmed on location without a traditional screenplay, its naturalistic performances heavily improvised by a cast of what at that time were B-movie actors—in form and content constituted a threat to "straight" society and Hollywood business as usual. *Love Story*—a sappy romance adapted from a book, made by a studio, and featuring beautiful, homogenous young stars, including Paramount chief Robert Evans' wife Ali Macgraw—was the epitome of "straight" Hollywood product. When it became an even bigger hit than *Easy Rider*, the studios had evidence that they could reach the youth audience after all, not by getting into business with upstarts, but merely by updating their sales tactics. Thus independent artists and mold-breaking movies like *Easy Rider* outlived their commercial usefulness.

"We blew it," says Peter Fonda's character in the film's second-to-last scene, an implicit acknowledgement of its makers' self-awareness of the limits and pitfalls of the counterculture. *Love Story* is the result of the counterculture's failure to produce permanent change, an emblem of the dominant culture waiting for the upstarts to burn themselves out, and then coming back stronger than ever.

Left: *Easy Rider* (1969).

Opposite page: Paul Le Mat in *American Graffiti* (1973).

current state, he said, the film was unreleasable. Coppola stood up for Lucas. He pulled out his checkbook on the spot and offered to buy the film back from Universal so that he could have it released through another distributor. Tanen demurred. But in the spring of that year, the Writers Guild of America went on strike, and Lucas and Coppola, both members, could not cross picket lines to enter the studio. In their absence, Universal shaved a few minutes off the film. Again, Lucas felt that the cuts hardly made the film better or more commercial—they only made it evident that it was the studios that really had the power, not the artists.

American Graffiti made $55.1 million at the US box office, and $117 million worldwide. Given its minuscule budget, it was the most profitable American film ever released to that date. Lucas personally made four million dollars. He and Coppola had a falling out on how to divide back end points on the grosses. After watching how much money Universal made on the movie—far more than Lucas's $4 million—Coppola became determined to finance future movies himself. The Zoetrope dream was born, and could only really survive, in the year-long climate of confusion between the surprise success of *Easy Rider* and the engineered success of *Love Story* (1970)—beginning when old Hollywood was forced to realize it didn't know how to serve the tastes of young masses, and ending when it proved it could figure it out.

Moving out of Coppola's shadow

With his *American Graffiti* windfall, Lucas purchased two Victorian-style houses in the Northern California neighborhood of San Anselmo. One was for he and Marcia to live in. The other, a few blocks away, would house the headquarters of Lucasfilm.

Up until the massive success of *American Graffiti*, Lucas was still acting as a subordinate to Coppola, described by William Friedkin as "one of those guys hanging around for scraps."[17] With the release of *Star Wars* in 1977, Lucas would move out of Coppola's shadow, but his friend and former mentor played a role in Lucas's defining blockbuster in two key, indirect ways. *The Godfather*—a film that Coppola didn't want to make, a for-hire project he took on for the money and only accidentally found a way to make his own—was the start of a new mentality in Hollywood, through which genre films could be "gentrified." No longer a niche, gangster films, horror flicks, and other former B-movie genres could now be expected to hit the kind of cultural nerve that would guarantee massive business. Lucas had played a key role in convincing Coppola to make the movie. When the project presented itself as a way of getting out of the financial hole he had dug for himself with Zoetrope, he asked Lucas for advice—should he take it? As usual, Lucas played pragmatist, telling his friend, "I don't see any choice."[18] And yet Lucas himself vowed to multiple parties that unlike Coppola, he would never "have to make

The Godfather"—meaning he would refuse to take a studio job primarily motivated by a need to pay the bills. If George Lucas was going to sell out, he was going to do it on his own terms.

If Coppola's "failure" inspired Lucas to take an opposite approach to business, Coppola made another major "gift" to Lucas's career by robbing his friend of a film he had planned to direct, *Apocalypse Now*. At height of the Vietnam War, Lucas and his USC classmate John Milius had conceived of a low-budget fiction film, first to be shot documentary style on the actual battlefield (an approach reminiscent to Haskell Wexler's *Medium Cool*, 1969), and later with rural California and the Philippines subbing for Southeast Asia. The project, so conceived with Milius writing, Lucas directing, and Coppola producing, had been wrapped up in Coppola's Zoetrope deal with Warners—meaning that, at the end of the day, Coppola controlled the property. Coppola, still smarting over his comparatively minimal profit on *American Graffiti*, proposed a deal that, had Lucas accepted it, would have forced

him, essentially, to direct the movie for free. Lucas refused to make the movie on those terms, which seemed to be what Coppola wanted—he could now direct *Apocalypse Now* himself.

When *The Godfather*'s box-office gross hit $100 million, Lucas accompanied Coppola to a Mercedes dealership to buy a limo. The lure of financial freedom would prove irresistible to the younger filmmaker. Coppola would admit later that with overnight success (and the attendant moral slipperiness that followed), at some point he started to feel like the great villain he had brought to the screen, Don Corleone. A similar parallel would be made decades later between Lucas and his great villainous creation, Darth Vader—not least by Lucas himself.

Charles Martin Smith
in *American Graffiti* (1973).

Opposite page: George Lucas
with Francis Ford Coppola
on the set of *Star Wars* (1977).

The first trilogy
Star Wars, The Empire Strikes Back, Return of the Jedi

Mark Hamill in *The Empire Strikes Back* (1980).

Once it was clear that Lucas's dreamed-of version of *Apocalypse Now* was not going to work out, the filmmaker transposed some of his basic ideas about the morals of war and rebellion into a script he began to call *The Star Wars*. But while certain elements grew out of a fascination with Vietnam, *Star Wars* was not intended to function as a parable to life on Earth circa 1977. Instead, Lucas wanted to tell a classic moral tale, set in a completely fantastic time and place—but fabricated expressly to look real.

"Westerns, mythology, and samurai movies"

Lucas struggled for years with the screenplay. The entire concept stemmed from his mental image of a dogfight in space, but in order to build a story around that image, Lucas consciously borrowed elements from all of his own favorite cultural products, mixing up the entertainments of his childhood with the more "respectable" cinematic references he picked up in San Francisco, from his friends, and from school.

While he was certainly aware of J.R.R. Tolkien's epics, he was more directly influenced by Frank Herbert's novel *Dune* (set on a desert planet, like *Star Wars*' Tattoine), the serialized novels of Edgar Rice Burroughs (particularly *John Carter of Mars*), Sir James George Fraser's comparative mythology study *The Golden Bough,* and Isaac Asimov's *Foundation* series and *Guide to the Bible.* As he worked through many drafts of the screenplay, Lucas was increasingly guided by the writings of mythologist Joseph Campbell, whose *The Hero With a Thousand Faces* inspired him to "make [the story] fit more into that classic mold." [19]

Lucas's cinematic references were more varied. Much more personally interested in the French New Wave's version of narrative storytelling than Hollywood's, Lucas still had a soft spot for the television he binged on as a kid, particularly the Flash Gordon space adventure serials. "We tried to buy the rights to *Flash Gordon* from King Features but the deal would have been prohibitive," producer Gary Kurtz said later. "They wanted too much money, too much control, so starting over and creating from scratch was the answer." [20]

Visually, there is an obvious debt to the realistic minimalism of space in *2001,* and to Fritz Lang's *Metropolis* (1927), which merged with Asimov's writing on robots in Lucas's mind, leading to the notion of C-3PO as an android with a point of view.

The relationship between C-3PO and his partner R2D2, and their function in the film as

comic-relief guides, was inspired by the two bumbling peasants on an epic journey in Akira Kurosawa's *The Hidden Fortress*. One draft of Lucas's script owed so much to Kurosawa's film in its theme and action that Lucas and Kurtz also briefly contemplated buying the remake rights to *The Hidden Fortress*. Lucas also drew some of *Star Wars*' look, characterizations, and hero quest elements from Westerns, particularly *A Fistful of Dollars* (1964, Sergio Leone's remake of Kurosawa's 1961 *Yojimbo*) and John Ford's *The Searchers* (1956), whose saloon scene directly inspired the Mos Aisley cantina sequence.

Star Wars was also very savvily designed as a commercial endeavor. Lucas saw it as a film for ten- to twelve-year olds. Disney had given up the older kids' market, and nothing had filled that void. And though he'd later boast that *Star Wars* was an insane gamble, Lucas was very consciously trying to engineer for the mainstream success of a Disney movie. "I put in all the elements that said, 'This is going to be a hit,'" Lucas admitted. [21]

Reinventing the fable

In its intentional moral didacticism, *Star Wars* was a strike against the ideas contained within so many New Hollywood films. Lucas thought someone needed to teach kids right from wrong, and he appointed himself the man to do it. But in order to do this in a way that would inspire youthful audiences rather than make them feel preached to (the way Lucas himself felt, watching the films of some of his peers), Lucas wanted to cast lessons in the palatable form of fables. "Rather than do some angry, socially relevant film," Lucas said, "I realized there was another relevance that is even more important—dreams and fantasies, getting children to believe there is more to life than garbage and killing … a whole generation was growing up without fairy tales." [22]

The only true analogues between the dream world of *Star Wars* and Lucas's own world were personal. The adventures of Luke—the bored, frustrated country bumpkin who gets swept up in a

Opposite page:
Top left: *Flash Gordon*
by Frederick Stephani (1936).
Bottom left: *Tora ! Tora ! Tora !*
by Richard Fleischer (1970).
Top right: *The Hidden Fortress*
by Akira Kurosawa (1958).
Bottom right: *Metropolis*
by Fritz Lang (1927).

Above top: *A Fistful of Dollars*
by Sergio Leone (1964).
Above bottom: *2001: A Space
Odyssey* by Stanley Kubrick
(1968).

rebellion against the established power, and ultimately has to confront his fearsome father—were not-so-thinly veiled versions of Lucas's own youth, growing up in the shadow of his intimidating father in sleepy Modesto, joining the ranks of the New Hollywood against the formidable Empire of Hollywood. The anti-hero character of Han Solo was invented as a gloss on Coppola, Lucas's partner and rival—a gambler who could save the day, but only by taking great risks. But the personal never overwhelmed the universal. Lucas knew that mining his own experiences for feel-good escapism had worked for *American Graffiti*. *Star Wars* would take it a step further, offering world-weary viewers a respite from their daily lives via a new myth, set in far-off lands created from scratch.

Lucas's visionary deal

American Graffiti was released in August 1973, and its massive success put Lucas in a strong position to negotiate. Unwilling to work again with Universal, whom he never forgave for imposing cuts on *American Graffiti* against his will, Lucas brought his Star Wars concept to Alan Ladd Jr at Fox. Newly installed as Head of Creative Affairs at the studio, Ladd was relatively young, and he was a big fan of *American Graffiti*. Eager to get into business with Lucas, he had offered a $3.5 million budget for *Star Wars*, and promised Lucas forty percent of the net profits. When *American Graffiti* exploded, Lucas renegotiated for more power. He insisted on producing the film through his newly launched company Lucasfilm, and demanded ownership of music rights and soundtrack profits, sequel rights, and merchandising rights. Ladd happily signed the rights over—at that point he had no reason to assume there'd be any real money in such ancillaries. Much about *Star Wars* would cause executives like Ladd to rethink everything they thought they knew.

"A long time ago in a galaxy far, far away ..."

Star Wars (retitled *Star Wars Episode IV: A New Hope* upon its first theatrical re-release in 1981) begins with this ten-word phrase, imposed in light blue over a solid black background, with no audio accompaniment. This was Lucas's way of giving viewers a moment to put their everyday reality and its attendant anxieties on pause so that they might better surrender to his fantasy. That fantasy is introduced with the first edit of the film, which is accompanied by the first crashing note of John Williams' score: the title *Star Wars*, in large yellow letters, appears in the center of a black screen sprinkled with the silver stars of Lucas's fictional galaxy and then recedes into space, followed by what has become known as "the opening crawl."

As the film's action will drop us about forty years in to what Lucas envisioned as a half-century-spanning drama, the explanatory text that crawls up the screen is crucial to get the viewer up to speed. This is how we learn that the wars of the title concern two factions: the evil Empire, which is building the Death Star, "an armored space station with enough power to destroy an entire planet"; and the idealistic, comparatively disadvantaged Rebel Alliance, which is operating from a hideout somewhere in the galaxy. What the text doesn't do is tell us how to identify the good guys from the bad, in terms of pure visuals. An opening space battle thus becomes almost abstract—two types of never-before-seen aircraft, both shooting lasers, before we've met a single character. In the same way that Lucas's student shorts sparked sensory responses rather than engage the viewer intellectually or emotionally with story, here, in presenting action before he's introduced characters, Lucas asks that we turn off intellectual instincts right away in order to be thrilled by the awesome spectacle of the battle itself.

It is not until several scenes into the film that we meet an identifiable human protagonist in the form of Princess Leia (Carrie Fisher), the beautiful, headstrong nineteen-year-old leader of the Rebel Alliance. She is glimpsed briefly recording a holographic cry for help into a dustbin-shaped robot (or "droid") called R2D2. Knowing she is about to be taken hostage by the Empire's imposing enforcer Darth Vader (voiced by James Earl Jones), Leia uploads to R2's memory bank the galaxy's greatest contraband: the blueprints for the in-construction Death Star. R2 and another robot, the gold-plated, gawky protocol droid C-3PO, crash-land on desert planet Tattoine. The arrival in Tattoine allows Lucas for the first time to indulge in classical photographic aesthetics: the vast widescreen vistas of

Star Wars (1977).

the desert planet recall the rumination on the natural beauty of the environment that he captured
in the short he made on the set of *MacKenna's Gold*.
These scenes, shot in Tunisia, shock the viewer out
of the high-speed, permanent midnight space opera
of the film's early scenes. It is not until Lucas settles
into a slightly more cinematically familiar environment that it becomes apparent just to what extent
the first act was carried by artificial constructs—
robot characters, model planes, an invented galaxy
that viewers had never before seen.

    Nearly every scene in this first film of the
series opens up new doors in the mythology. On
Tattoine, the two droids are sold to the step-uncle
of a frustrated teenager named Luke Skywalker
(Mark Hamill). An orphan who is desperately curi-
ous about where he comes from, Luke longs to
travel, to find adventure and himself. Soon Luke
discovers the holographic message hidden on the
droid, with the beautiful Leia pleading, "Help me,

Carrie Fisher and Kenny Baker
in *Star Wars* (1977).

Opposite page: Anthony Daniels,
Mark Hamill, and Alec Guinness
in *Star Wars* (1977).

Obi-Wan Kenobi. You're my only hope." Obi-Wan (Alec Guinness) turns out to be Ben Kenobi, who Luke knows as the local hermit. Obi-Wan confides that he fought alongside Luke's father, Anakin Skywalker, decades earlier. The two were Jedi knights, members of an elite squad of peacekeepers who drew power and strength from a mysterious, spiritual source known as the Force. Kenobi claims Anakin was killed by Darth Vader, another Jedi who turned to the Dark Side—meaning he began to use the Force for evil rather than good. Fully aware of the danger Princess Leia Organa of Alderaan and her rebel movement are in from the Empire, Obi-Wan agrees to help her, and invites Luke to accompany him on the journey and to learn the ways of the Jedi as they travel.

Luke, Obi-Wan, and the droids travel to Mos Eisley, a trading portal and transport hub, where the plan is to find a ship that can take them to Alderaan. In a cantina, Obi-Wan goes to look for a pilot and leaves Luke alone at the bar. Surrounded by varieties of alien species that would be scary for their foreignness even if they weren't knocking back large quantities of space booze, the small, frail Luke recoils with anxiety and discomfort. It's a fascinating, surreal scene, emulating what the small, frail, sober, introvert Lucas must have felt in hard-partying, *Easy Rider*-era Hollywood. Here, forty minutes into the movie, we meet Han Solo (Harrison Ford) for the first time. In our introduction to Han in the cantina, he's having a dispute with Greedo, an alien bounty hunter who works for crime lord Jabba the Hutt. With a blaster gun pointed at Han, Greedo snarls, "I've been waiting for this for a long time"—implying that he's going to kill Han, who can't pay a debt he owes Jabba. Before Greedo can fire, Han says, "I bet you have," and fires a lethal shot from his own gun, which he's been hiding under the table.

For a price, Han agrees to fly Obi-Wan, Luke, and the Droids to rescue Leia in the Millennium

Falcon, the beater of a spacecraft he uses for smuggling. On the ship, Obi-Wan begins training Luke in the ways of the Force, teaching him how to use a lightsaber and giving him commands to "stretch out with your feelings." Han dismisses the ways of the Jedi as a racket of "hokey religions and ancient weapons." Patting his blaster, he says, "No mystical energy field controls MY destiny." This philosophical difference is key to Lucas's conception of the Star Wars series as a coming-of-age story, in which Luke will have to determine what kind of man he's going to become and what value system he's going to use to navigate a violent, unfair world.

After spending the first half of the film slowly, even methodically, introducing the world and its characters, Lucas gives over the second half of the film to action set pieces—chase sequences in space and on the maze-like deck of the Death Star, in which an obstacle is presented just so our heroes can figure out how to circumvent it. The story is not always easily comprehensible—Lucas refuses to slow down the pace to allow a viewer to catch up—but the imagery is rarely less than stunning. As a visualist, Lucas thrills to the abstract beauty of action: the non-dialogue scenes are a visual symphony of lights, sparks, clouds of smoke punctuated by laser shards. The blasts and explosions are gorgeous, multicolored balls of fire.

Throughout all of this action, one of Lucas's main goals is to sow the seeds of a love triangle between the boyish Luke, the roguish Han, and business-like beauty Leia. He also sets up the relationships between Obi-Wan, Darth Vader, and Luke. Obi-Wan and Darth Vader—once mentor and protégé—meet for the first time in decades and engage in a lightsaber fight. "If you strike me down," Obi-Wan warns his now-evil former friend, "I shall become more powerful than you can possibly imagine." Vader does strike down Obi Wan, whose body vanishes. In the film's final dogfight, Luke is cornered by Vader. When all seems lost, Han Solo—who previously left the rebels to their own devices—returns, and from the Falcon fires at Vader's wingmen to give Luke a clear shot at the Death Star. Guided by the ghostly voice of Obi-Wan to "use the Force," Luke hits his target, and the Empire's base is destroyed.

Over the course of a single film, Luke has gained and lost a father figure in Obi-Wan and an older-brother role model—and rival—in Han Solo. He's had both a spiritual and moral awakening, and in the Rebellion, he has found his tribe. In a sense, the film is Lucas's own experience of leaving home, writ large and transposed to space.

Industrial Light and Magic: inventing the future

Star Wars was shot in the summer of 1976, on location in Tunisia, and on sound stages at Shepperton Studios in England. The sites were selected for their proximity to Hollywood: Lucas wanted to get as far away from the eyes of Fox as possible. Producer Gary Kurtz chose the British crew, which included cinematographer Gill Taylor (whose previous credits

Opposite page: David Prowse and Carrie Fisher in *Star Wars* (1977).

Mark Hamill in *Star Wars* (1977).

"How are we going to do this?"

Though his partnership with George Lucas was short-lived, special effects director John Dykstra would play a huge role in helping the filmmaker realize the groundbreaking imagery of the Star Wars films. After working on optical and model effects on Douglas Trumbull's directorial debut *Silent Running* (1972), Dykstra, who had a degree in industrial design, was hired by a city planning initiative in Northern California to create short films visualizing hypothetical city designs using small models. It was on that project that Dykstra started exploring the possibilities of using a computer to control a camera's motion. When Trumbull turned down Lucas's offer to head the special effects department on *Star Wars*, Lucas hired Dykstra instead. Dykstra remembered in 2008, "We kind of walked into an empty warehouse and sat on the floor and went 'how are we going to do this?'" The answer to that question was Dykstraflex—a computerized rig, built from obsolete VistaVision cameras, which could be programmed to repeat specific paths of motion around miniature models, allowing the artists to build complicated effects shots in layers using optical printing. Dykstra and his collaborators, Alvah J. Miller and Jerry Jeffress, won a special Oscar for the Dykstraflex accomplishment.

Lucas the perfectionist was less impressed than the Academy. He was frustrated over the time and money spent on effects that he considered to be barely usable, and suspicious that Dykstra had spent too much of the film's budget developing the camera that now bore his name. While other technicians who worked on *Star Wars* moved up to Marin County to the new offices of Industrial Light and Magic, Dykstra stayed behind and formed his own effects company, Apogee. "Truth be known, I don't think George wanted me up there," Dykstra remembered later. "I think George wanted people who were more willing to develop a company, and I wasn't that much a company guy. I mean, like an administrator." Apogee's first project was the original Battlestar Galactica, which Lucas considered to be a Star Wars rip-off. Dykstra went on to supervise effects for many Hollywood blockbusters, including Tim Burton's *Batman* (1989) and Sam Raimi's *Spider-Man 2* (2004), for which he won another Oscar.

John Dykstra on the set of *Star Wars* (1977).

Opposite page: *Star Wars* (1977).

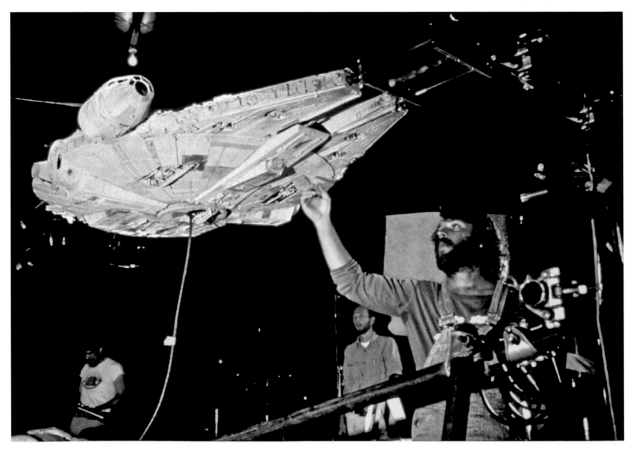

42

included *Dr. Strangelove* and *A Hard Day's Night,* both 1964) and production designer John Barry, who had worked on Kubrick's *A Clockwork Orange* (1971). A homebody slow to socialize with new people, Lucas was out of his element in England. He was notoriously cold with actors, and known to give minimal direction. After a take, he'd say, "Same thing, only better." The problem was exacerbated by the fact that the human characters like Luke interacted with characters like C-3P0 and Darth Vader who were played by actors in transformative suits and masks, with voices dubbed in later.

Meanwhile, back in the States, work was underway to conceptualize and create *Star Wars*' groundbreaking special effects. For the most part, Hollywood studios were trying to get out of the business of maintaining full-service backlots, and had shut down their effects houses accordingly. Industrial Light and Magic—the Lucas-owned company that would dominate the emerging CGI trade in the coming years—was born out of the *Star Wars* team's need to figure out how to realize Lucas's

vision without the aid of studio infrastructure. Lucas tried to hire Douglas Trumbull, the special effects wizard who had created the space imagery of *2001: A Space Odyssey* (1968), but he declined the job. Instead, Lucas was able to get Trumbull's assistant, John Dykstra. Dykstra and a small crew moved into a warehouse in the northern Los Angeles suburb of Van Nuys, and got to work creating a special effects revolution from scratch.

With money tight, the newly established ILM largely relied on building what it needed out of archaic, discarded equipment. The spaceships themselves were built from model kits and toys. It wasn't the only way in which the team cobbled together their brave new world out of what journalist Stephen Zito would call "the usable past."[23] Lucas conceptualized the space battle scenes by editing together bits of dogfights shot off the TV. "Every time there was a war movie on TV, like *The Bridges at Toko-Ri*, I would watch it—and if there was a dogfight sequence, I would videotape it," Lucas has said. "It was really a way of getting a sense of

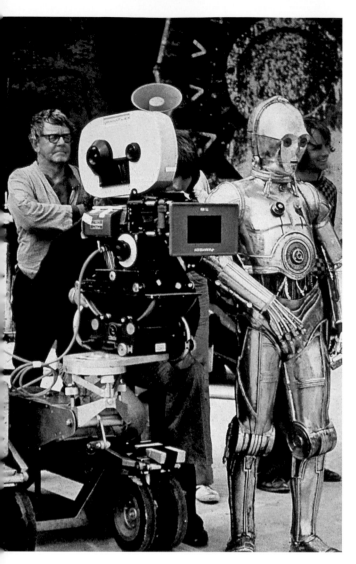

Anthony Daniels (on the right) in *Star Wars* (1977).

the movement of the spaceships."[24] Other films represented in that reel: Richard Fleischer's *Tora! Tora! Tora!* (1970), Guy Hamilton's *The Battle of Britain* (1969), Josef von Sternberg's *Jet Pilot* (1957), Walter Grauman's *633 Squadron* (1964), and Michael Anderson's *The Dam Busters* (1955), which Lucas would directly reference in the staging and dialogue of his film's final air-fight sequence.[25]

In order to realistically copy that movement using miniature crafts, Lucas showed his compilation of dogfights to Dykstra, who in turn created a computer-controlled animation camera that could repeat the exact same motion over and over again as different models were moved in and out of the frame. Painted backdrops defining the galaxy and animated laser fire were layered in later. Using the principles of animation, they created the illusion of hyperreal live action. "The film has to make us believe it really existed," Lucas said, "that we've really gone to another galaxy to shoot [it.]"[26]

For a year, they didn't have a single usable shot, even though they had spent at least $4 million—more than the original budget for the entire movie. Even in the end, ILM wasn't able to produce prolonged shots, only short scraps of each effect, meaning Lucas and his editors (Marcia Lucas, once again) had to cut quickly between discrete effects shots. These constraints dictated the film's rhythm, particularly in the flight sequences, which are edited so rapidly the viewer is overwhelmed by the action—and unable to spot the seams.

On its initial release in May 1977, *Star Wars* would become the highest grossing film of all time, but during its production, Lucas's intimates hardly treated him as a king-to-be. The first friends-and-family screening, held in early 1977 at the Lucas home in San Anselmo, was a disaster. At dinner afterward, Brian De Palma was merciless. "You've left the audience out," the *Carrie* director warned Lucas. "They don't know what's going on."[27] In a way, his criticism nailed the braveness of Lucas's approach, which prizes visual stimulation over traditional narrative storytelling, and begins in the middle of the action and doesn't stop to allow the viewer to get caught up. Only Steven Spielberg got it, promising studio executive Alan Ladd that the movie would make at least $35 million.

Star Wars would eventually surpass Spielberg's *Jaws* (1975) as the biggest money-maker of all time.

Mark Hamill, Carrie Fisher, and Harrison Ford in *Star Wars* (1977)

Lucas became an instant millionaire, and started trading "points" on the film's profits as currency. In his frustration over the stress caused by the effects, he didn't offer extra points to John Dykstra, who in turn started his own company, poaching most of ILM's staff. Lucas moved the stragglers who were left up to a new facility in Marin County, the Northern California countryside that would become the locus of his budding empire.

The serialization of Star Wars

Directing *Star Wars* had literally made George Lucas sick. He had worked himself into a state of exhaustion and depression; he suffered from chest pains and hypertension and the effects of diabetes. Physically wrecked by the shoot, he decided he'd never direct again. But the Star Wars franchise was just beginning, and he had no intention of giving up control. Lucas's contract dictated that if he didn't start working on a *Star Wars* sequel within two years after the first film's release, the sequel rights would revert back to the studio. So before 1977 was out, he had begun assembling a crew to make *The Empire Strikes Back* (1980).

There is some debate as to whether or not Lucas always intended for *Star Wars* to encompass more than one film, let alone three or six. Some have suggested that he expanded his conception of 45 the wider Star Wars universe and mythology only after the first film became a hit and the studio hungered for sequels. But there is evidence that, if Lucas didn't necessarily set out to make a six-film series starting with the fourth film, he did envision the events of *A New Hope* to occur in the chronological middle of a much more expansive saga. In 1980, Lucas recalled that the serialization of the series stemmed from his attempt to make his unwieldy first draft of the screenplay manageable: "I wanted to make a fairy tale epic, but this was like *War and Peace*. So I took that script and cut it in half, put the first half aside and decided to write the screenplay from the second half. I was on page 170, and I thought, 'Holy smokes, I need 100 pages, not 500,' but I had all these great scenes. So I took that story and cut it into three parts. I took the first part and said, 'This will be my script. But

no matter what happens, I am going to get these three movies made.'" [28]

A new reality

By the time we meet him again in *The Empire Strikes Back* (1980), Luke has become a commander of the Rebel Alliance's leaders, stationed on the ice planet of Hoth alongside Leia and the once-reluctant Rebel Han Solo. Luke is attacked in a snowstorm by a beast called a Wampa. He loses consciousness and has a vision of his late mentor Obi-Wan Kenobi, who tells him to go to the Dagobah System to learn the ways of the Jedi from a master called Yoda.

Since the events of the first film, Darth Vader has become obsessed with capturing Luke. To that end, he leads the Empire in a battle to destroy Hoth. In what had by then become a template for films in the Star Wars series, this battle

Carrie Fisher in *The Empire Strikes Back* by Irvin Kershner (1980).

offers viewers a major sensory spectacle before the story of the film really begins. Following the battle, Luke takes off to find Yoda. He's surprised to find that the great Jedi who trained Obi Wan Kenobi is in fact an ancient alien (voiced by Frank Oz), no more than a couple of feet high.

The design and production of Yoda posed a number of challenges. Lucas asked his character-creation crew, led by Ralph McQuarrie and Joe Johnston (later the director of such special-effects blockbusters as *Honey, I Shrunk the Kids* and *Captain America*), to avoid making the small, vaguely humanoid creature reminiscent of any specific ethnic group. Jim Henson, creator of The Muppets, was called in to bring the green, 800-year-old Jedi master to life. Working with a twenty-eight-inch animatronic whose moving features were controlled from below, Lucas and Henson spent a year

refining the character's look. The vision they ultimately settled on—though undeniably aged, otherworldly, and elfin—was heavily inspired by Albert Einstein. There were several versions of Yoda that could be operated with rods, through radio control, or worn on the arm of voice actor/puppeteer Frank Oz, depending on what the shot required. The key materials were foam latex covered in natural hair— each strand hand-sewn using hypodermic needles.

The bulk of the film's middle act shuttles back and forth between Luke's often hallucinatory Jedi training with Yoda and the rest of the gang's flight from Vader. Ultimately they all end up in the same trap. Vader freezes Han Solo in a block of carbonite to be delivered into the hands of Jabba the Hutt, and then Luke engages Vader in a spectacular lightsaber duel. With one swift move, Vader cuts off Luke's hand, then intones, "Luke, I am your

Mark Hamill in *The Empire Strikes Back* by Irvin Kershner (1980).

father." The dark lord invites his Rebel son to join forces with him, to put an end to the fighting so that together they can rule the galaxy. Luke refuses, and jumps down an air shaft. He telepathically calls out to Leia—who, for reasons he can't yet understand, hears him, and mobilizes a rescue.

Considered by many fans to be the best film in the series, *The Empire Strikes Back* certainly has some of the most beautiful imagery of the first three films. Kershner's aerial shots of the cloudy ice planet imbue the place with mystery, and the design of the swamps suggests the team is pushing way beyond the first film's mash-up of "Westerns, mythology and samurai movies"—here, they're inventing new landscapes, new forms, a new reality.

Men versus machines

Increasingly, there's less focus on the humans than the machines, which have a certain majesty and scale, while still betraying a shabbiness that you rarely see in filmed science fiction. The Rebels' ships, bases, and weapons actually look used. It was at Lucas's insistence that rust and grease be visible on the machines used by his heroes, in order to exaggerate the contrast between their rag-tag brand and the well-funded but thoroughly evil Empire.

There's much in the film to suggest that Lucas was grappling with criticisms that he lacked a certain human sensitivity. At one point, the beloved droid C-3P0 grumbles, "Sometimes I just don't understand human behavior. I'm just trying to do my job …" *The Empire Strikes Back* also drops seeds of sympathy for Vader, who is part man and part machine himself. Frustrated by his human soldiers, Vader vows, "You have failed me for the last time."

That is perhaps how Lucas felt after working with Irvin Kershner, a journeyman with experience in many B-genres, and a former professor of Lucas's at USC, who was hired to direct *The Empire Strikes Back*. Lucas had trouble ceding control. "I come from the filmmakers' school of doing movies, which means I do everything myself," he said shortly after shooting *Star Wars*. "It's very hard for me to get into another system where everybody does things for me, and I say, "Fine."[29] Kershner, who didn't like and didn't understand special effects,

David Prowse and Mark Hamill in *The Empire Strikes Back* by Irvin Kershner (1980).

Carrie Fisher in *Return of the Jedi*
by Richard Marquand (1983).

Opposite page: David Prowse (on the left) in
Return of the Jedi by Richard Marquand (1983).

Following pages: *Return of the Jedi*
by Richard Marquand (1983).

went over budget and over schedule; the movie cost
three times as much as *Star Wars*. At one point, after
seeing an assembly edit, Lucas reportedly threw a
tantrum, raging to Kershner, "You're ruining my
movie!"[30] Lucas then took over shooting and editing reshoots himself. He could almost not afford
not to: he had put everything he had into the film.

From dark to light

Ultimately, Lucas's control-freak behavior paid off:
he made so much money on *The Empire Strikes Back*'s
blockbuster success that he finally became independent of the studios. The film cost $25 million
to make, paid for by *Star Wars* profits. Lucasfilm
made $92 million from it, which more than paid
for the $32.5 million budget of *Return of the Jedi*.
After what happened with Kershner on *The Empire
Strikes Back*, Lucas didn't want to leave anything

to chance. He hired Welsh director Richard Marquand, whose undistinguished credits and lack of
power made him perfect for the job: he would do
what Lucas told him to do and, as a non-union for-
eigner, he'd do it cheaply. Lucas was not going to be
a hands-off producer on what was then assumed
to be the final production of a trilogy. In mid-Jan-
uary 1982, he moved to London for the duration
of the shoot.

As the film opens, the Empire is building
a new ship more powerful than the Death Star.
Meanwhile, Han Solo is still frozen in a carbonite block in Jabba the Hutt's lair. A disguised
Leia makes an attempt to free Han and manages
to thaw him out, but is soon found out, and is
imprisoned herself. Jabba keeps her as his personal
slave, wrapped in chains and dressed in a gold
bikini. Jabba clearly represents Lucas's idea of total

power: it's gluttonous, disgusting, literally monstrous. That the much smaller Leia is the one to kill him, strangling him to death with the chains he put her in, is one with the trilogy's larger metaphor regarding the little guy triumphing over the behemoths. Yoda is dying, and Luke goes to visit his mentor on his deathbed. The pupil is nervous about the state of his training, but Yoda is adamant that the only thing left for Luke to do is to confront Vader one more time. Luke also learns that Leia is his twin sister—she heard his cry for help at the end of *The Empire Strikes Back* because the Force is strong within her, too.

Much of the film takes place on the forest moon of Endor, which is populated by a tribe of small, furry characters called Ewoks. While Leia, Han, and the Ewoks prepare to fight the Imperial forces, Luke goes to meet Vader, following Yoda's death-bed urging, hoping to bring out the buried good in his father. It's not as simple as that: Vader still hopes his son will join him on the Dark Side, and he delivers Luke to Emperor Palpatine (Ian McDiarmid) accordingly. When Luke refuses Palpatine's entreaty to cross over to the Dark Side, Palpatine summons the power of the Force to strike Luke with telepathic lightning. This shocks Vader into action: to save his son, he kills the Emperor, but is struck by lightning in the process. As he lies dying, Vader asks Luke to remove his mask, and Luke and Anakin Skywalker meet at last.

The Empire Strikes Back takes the Star Wars mythology into the realm of the gothic: Luke's journey of self-discovery, to confront his own dark side, is made literal. *Return of the Jedi* is a journey from dark to light. Perhaps too light: much of the film is devoted to the B-story involving the Ewoks, which seems like a distraction away from the core drama between a Force-crazed Luke and the slowly humanized Vader—as well as a blatant ploy to advertise toys.

The darker elements of the Star Wars trilogy are essentially neutralized by its end. In the final scene of the original trilogy, Vader, Yoda, and Obi-Wan unite as holograms beamed from Heaven, smiling and waving their blessings at the once rebellious kids, who have become the establishment. At some point, *Jedi* was intended to be a darker film, but before production began Lucas decided that a happy ending was non-negotiable. His insistence on moving in that direction caused a permanent riff with his producer, Gary Kurtz. "We had an outline and George changed everything in it," Kurtz said in 2010. "Instead of bittersweet and poignant he wanted a euphoric ending with everybody happy. The original idea was that they would recover [the kidnapped] Han Solo in the early part of story and that he would then die in the middle part of the film in a raid on an Imperial base. George then decided he didn't want any of the principals killed. By that time there were really big toy sales and that was a reason."[31]

Harrison Ford, Carrie Fisher, and Peter Mayhew
in *Return of the Jedi* by Richard Marquand (1983).

Influence and independence

The impact of the Star Wars series on filmmaking, as an art and as an industry, was massive and instant. For the most part, it was Hollywood that benefited, not the young Turks with whom Lucas came up or the experimental filmmakers with whom he claimed to feel the closest affinity.

Why was *Star Wars* so huge? For one thing, the first film benefited from a cultural move away from the radicalism of the '60s, which Lucas was not alone in pegging as "exhausting." It also anticipated the conservatism of the 1980s: patriotic and simpleminded, the series reestablished movies as something the whole family could enjoy together, rather than just another aspect of generational war. Lucas's notion of "pure cinema" as based on image and feeling, rather

than ideas and plot, invited viewers to experience cinema the way they did in the "old" days, rather than read it critically. There was no subtext to separate from the text; there was barely any text.

While most reviews were positive, Pauline Kael, in her very negative critique of *Star Wars*, made the compelling argument that the film's "special, huge success" was due to the way it both appealed to the senses of a very young audience and made older viewers feel like kids. "The loudness, the smash-and-grab editing, the relentless pacing drive every idea from your head; for young audiences Star Wars is like getting a box of Cracker Jack which is all prizes," Kael wrote. "The excitement of those who call it the film of the year goes way past nostalgia to the feeling that now is the time to return to childhood." [32]

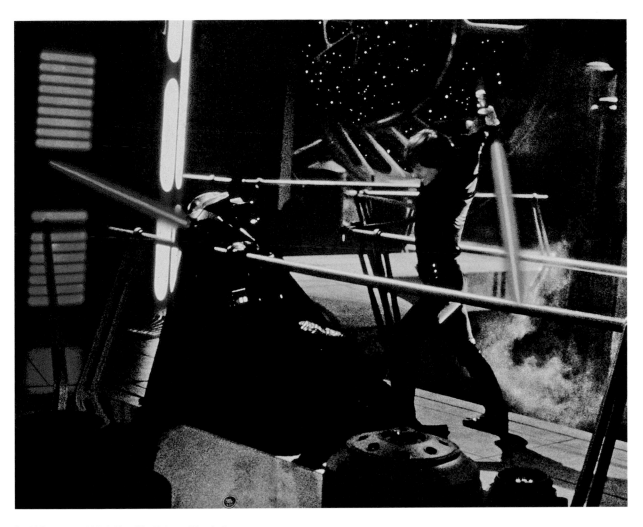

David Prowse and Mark Hamill in *Return of the Jedi*
by Richard Marquand (1983).

The technical innovation, and the new aesthetic options opened up by the technologies pioneered for the franchise were perhaps the series' biggest accomplishment. The computer-controlled moving cameras developed by John Dykstra and the team at ILM set a new standard for transient points of view in action and fantasy films, allowing models and miniatures to be filmed with greater verisimilitude. The original Star Wars films are, if nothing else, an incredible feat in the field of practical special effects—ironic, considering that Lucas and ILM would go on to pioneer the digital technologies that would all but destroy the art of practical effects in Hollywood movies.

In the short term, *Star Wars* finished the work begun by early blockbusters like *Jaws*, in the sense that it helped to turn Hollywood from an industry producing many types of products in many genres into an industry hellbent on reaching all segments of a mass audience with large-scale spectaculars, and reaping in countless ancillary monetary streams from toys and other tie-in merchandise. The films also helped to establish science fiction, previously considered a fringe interest and fodder for mostly B movies, as a legitimate mainstream movie genre.

In the long term, *Star Wars*, by opening the door for the big-budget, mass-market *auteur* film, undoubtedly paved the way for studios to take chances on funding expensive, ambitious films and franchises such as Robert Zemeckis' *Back to the Future* (1985), Tim Burton's and Christopher Nolan's

Batman films, Peter Jackson's *Lord of the Rings* (2001–3) series, and James Cameron's *Avatar* (2009). But the influence goes beyond the special effects or science-fiction realms: *Star Wars* can fairly be said to have influenced an entire generation of filmmakers (including Richard Kelly, Richard Linklater, Edgar Wright, and Kevin Smith, who famously included a debate about the comparative quality of *The Empire Strikes Back* and *Return of the Jedi* in his screenplay for *Clerks*) simply by awakening them, at a very young age, to the notion that in cinema, anything is possible.

Lucas, well aware that he had catapulted himself into a new league, made a number of arrogant moves proving just how little he felt he needed Hollywood's institutions. Most significantly, Lucas didn't want Kershner's director's credit at the beginning of *The Empire Strikes Back*. The DGA and WGA fined him, and in response, Lucas quit the guilds, resigned from the Academy, closed Lucasfilms' Los Angeles office, and moved what was left of his Southern California operations up to Northern California. There, construction on Skywalker Ranch was just beginning. "The union doesn't care about its members," Lucas fumed two years later. "It cares about making fancy rules that sound good on paper and are totally impractical." [33]

Over the following decade, far away from Hollywood, Lucas would set to work developing new technologies and processes that would make it possible for him to skirt Hollywood's rules for the rest of his career.

Harrison Ford in *Return of the Jedi* by Richard Marquand (1983).

Opposite page: Carrie Fisher and Harrison Ford in *Return of the Jedi* by Richard Marquand (1983).

The Spielberg years

Indiana Jones and Lucas's hiatus from directing

Harrison Ford in *Indiana Jones and the Temple of Doom* by Steven Spielberg (1984).

As both co-editor of George's movies and a frank but caring sounding board for his ideas, Marcia Lucas had been a crucial collaborator on *American Graffiti* and the Star Wars movies, as well as *Raiders of the Lost Ark* (1981). In June of 1982, the Lucases announced they would divorce. As the couple had not signed a pre-nuptial agreement, under California law Marcia was entitled to fifty percent of her ex-husband's assets. It was one of the largest divorce settlements in California history at that time. The repercussions of the divorce would be felt throughout the next decade—personally, emotionally, professionally, and financially. But Marcia's absence was arguably felt just as strongly in Lucas's creative work in the period after the first *Star Wars* trilogy and before the prequels. Whether or not it had anything to do with being left by his editor and wife, there's no question the boy wonder whose unparalleled streak of success spanning *American Graffiti*, the Star Wars films, and the beginning of the Indiana Jones franchise was soon in for a sharp comedown. Though Lucas didn't direct a film between *A New Hope* in 1977 and *Star Wars Episode 1: The Phantom Menace* in 1999, he consistently worked through the 1980s and '90s—writing, producing, financing, inventing. But he was somewhat "off the grid."

Collaborating with Spielberg

Flashback to May 1977: the weekend that *Star Wars* had opened in US theaters, George and Marcia had headed to Maui for an extended vacation with their old friends Willard Huyck and Gloria Katz. The trip had been planned for months as a way to get George out of town so he wouldn't obsess over box-office numbers and reviews. No one was more surprised than the director himself when *Star Wars*'s stunning box office made the evening news. Spielberg called to congratulate George and then, at Lucas's invitation, Spielberg and his girlfriend, actress Amy Irving, got on a plane to join the group on vacation.

Spielberg was aware that, to rebels such as Coppola and Lucas, he represented "the establishment." While they were fighting to get Zoetrope off the ground and keep it from falling apart, Spielberg acknowledged later, "I was being raised and nurtured inside Universal Studios ... I was working inside the system." [34]. Over a few days spent building a massive sandcastle on the beach, Spielberg went to work, convincing Lucas to join him on the inside. Spielberg recognized in Lucas the same ambition he himself had, to make mainstream movies for mass audiences, but to be able to do it his way, without interference from studio suits. The only way to make that happen was to finance the movies independently. Of all the ambitious young men in Hollywood, this was something that only Spielberg, after *Jaws*, and Lucas, after *Star Wars*, had the clout and capital to pull off. Lucas, determined to avoid the traps that his former mentor Francis Ford Coppola had fallen into, was a receptive audience.

Soon Lucas and Spielberg were discussing a collaboration. As far back as 1973, Lucas had been toying around with a character he called Indiana Smith (Indiana was the name of Marcia's dog). With director and writer Philip Kaufman, one of his Northern California compatriots, Lucas had sketched out an action-adventure, period piece about an archeologist with a double life—part academic, part swashbuckler, part Cary Grant-like playboy—who, at Kaufman's suggestion, went on a mission to find the Ark of the Covenant. A few years later, there on the beach, Lucas and Spielberg continued to brainstorm this new kind of action hero. Spielberg, who wanted to add to the character a touch of Humphrey Bogart from John Huston's *Treasure of Sierra Madre* (1948), said his main concern was the name. And so Indiana Smith became Indiana Jones, hero of *Raiders of the Lost Ark*.

A film made by voracious movie fans

Spielberg hired Lawrence Kasdan to write *Raiders of the Lost Ark* based on the quality of an un-produced script, *Continental Divide* (Kasdan would also do crucial rewrites on *The Empire Strikes Back*, which Lucas was developing at the same time). Kasdan, Lucas, and Spielberg sat in Kasdan's house every day for two weeks, spitballing ideas into a tape recorder. Kasdan had the tapes transcribed and turned them into a screenplay. In the process, he shifted the conception of Indy more toward his own icon of old-movie manhood: Clark Gable.

Raiders of the Lost Ark (1981) opens in 1936, in Peru, with Indiana Jones (Harrison Ford) liberating a fertility idol from an ancient tomb. The idol ends up in the hands of René Belloq (Paul Freeman), Indy's nefarious rival archeologist. Indy returns to his university post in the States, where he learns that Adolf Hitler is looking for the Ark of the Covenant, which he believes has occult powers that could make the Nazi army invincible. Indy's old

George Lucas with Steven Spielberg on the set of *Raiders of the Lost Ark* by Steven Spielberg (1981).

Opposite page: Amrish Puri (center) in *Indiana Jones and the Temple of Doom* (1984).

Karen Allen and Harrison Ford in *Raiders of the Lost Ark* by Steven Spielberg (1981).

mentor, Abner Ravenswood, is believed to have the Staff of Ra, another artifact that holds the clues to the Ark of the Covenant's location. In the hopes of getting his hands on the Ark before Hitler does, Indy heads to Nepal, where he finds the Staff of Ra now belongs to Abner's daughter Marion (Karen Allen), Indy's ex-girlfriend. She accompanies the rogue archeologist on his globetrotting mission.

The film was a massive hit, grossing $50 million in its first month of release (nearly $120 million, adjusted for inflation). Like *Star Wars*, *Raiders of the Lost Ark* had been made by voracious movie fans who, in some sense, aimed simply to make a kind of highlight reel of the genre elements they loved, ratcheted up to a modern speed through special effects and editing. While many critics were on board with this approach ("It wants only to entertain," wrote

Roger Ebert at the end of a breathlessly admiring review. "It succeeds."[35]), one notable naysayer was Pauline Kael. Having helped to usher in the New Hollywood generation through her rave review of *Bonnie and Clyde* in 1967, Kael used her *Raiders of the Lost Ark* review to forcefully express dismay over what she suggested was a newer wave, primarily motivated by the demands of marketing. "You don't have time to breathe—or to enjoy yourself much, either. It's an encyclopedia of high spots from the old serials, run through at top speed and edited like a great trailer—for flash," Kael wrote. "It's a shocker when the big-time directors provide a rationale for the marketing division—when they say, as Spielberg does, that 'the real movie-lovers are still children.' And there's no doubt he means that in a congratulatory sense. The whole collapsing industry is being

Harrison Ford in *Raiders of the Lost Ark*
by Steven Spielberg (1981).

inspired by old Saturday-afternoon serials, and the
three biggest American moviemakers [Lucas, Spielberg and Coppola] are hooked on technological play-
things and techniques."

The critic saved her deepest disappointment
for Lucas. If he "weren't hooked on the crap of his
childhood—if he brought his resources to bear on
some projects with human beings in them—there's
no imagining the result. (There might be miracles.)"
But that won't happen, Kael concluded, because
"George Lucas is in the toy business." [36]

Doom and gloom

Raiders' financial success meant that a sequel was all
but inevitable. But in the interim between *Raiders of
the Lost Ark*'s release in 1981 and *Indiana Jones and the
Temple of Doom*'s premiere in 1984, both Lucas and

Spielberg experienced major traumas that dimmed
their perspective. Lucas was reeling from the sep-
aration from Marcia, and what he perceived as her
betrayal. Spielberg, meanwhile, had just had his
first brush with catastrophic scandal, when three
actors, including two children, were killed when
a stunt went wrong on the set of the Spielberg-
produced *Twilight Zone: The Movie* (1983).

That their respective depressions were sur-
facing in their collaboration was apparent to their
friends and would-be collaborators. Lawrence Kasdan turned down Lucas's offer to write the script.
"I didn't want to be associated with *Temple of Doom*,"
he said later, positing that the film "represents a
chaotic period in both their lives, and the movie
is very ugly and mean spirited." [37] Instead, Lucas
turned to his old friends Willard Huyck and Gloria

Katz to write a screenplay. Recycling story beats and set-pieces from the pre-*Raiders* brainstorming session, the couple wrote a prequel beginning in 1935. *The Temple of Doom* has Indiana Jones (again played by Harrison Ford) entrapped by a cult, whose perversion of Hindi mythology leads to child slavery and ritual sacrifice.

In *The Temple of Doom*, Indy's antihero ambiguity—the same thing that made Ford so appealing as Han Solo—was pushed to questionable extremes. Under the mind-control of the cult, Indy comes close to killing his love interest, played by Kate Capshaw, by dipping her body into a pit of hot lava. The film as a whole is markedly grotesque, never more so than when, in a human sacrifice scene, the cult's evil priest Mola Ram reaches his hand into a live body's chest and pulls out the still-beating human heart.

In her negative review of *Raiders*, Pauline Kael had quipped, "You can almost feel Lucas and Spielberg whipping the editor to clip things sharper—to move ahead." In fact, this was a fair summary of Lucas's function on *Temple of Doom*. As producer, Lucas pushed for this second film in the series to exploit a loosening of boundaries in terms of graphic content. The envelope was being pushed in the horror genre, which was becoming increasingly mainstream, not least with the Spielberg-produced *Poltergeist* (directed by Tobe Hopper, director of *The Texas Chainsaw Massacre*). Lucas urged Spielberg that they needed to up the rapidly escalating expectations of an audience they helped to create. Lucas literally pushed editor Michael Kahn to cut faster. The result was a film that moved frantically from one set-piece to the next, with plenty of spectacle and little emphasis on character. Even Spielberg eventually became concerned that they had gone too far. "I wasn't happy with *Temple of Doom* at all," he said in 1989. "It was too dark, too subterranean, and much too horrific. I thought it out-poltered *Poltergeist*. There's not an ounce of my own personal feeling in *Temple of Doom*." [38] In the United States, the film was originally rated PG. After an outcry from parents who felt it was way too violent for younger kids, Spielberg lobbied the MPAA

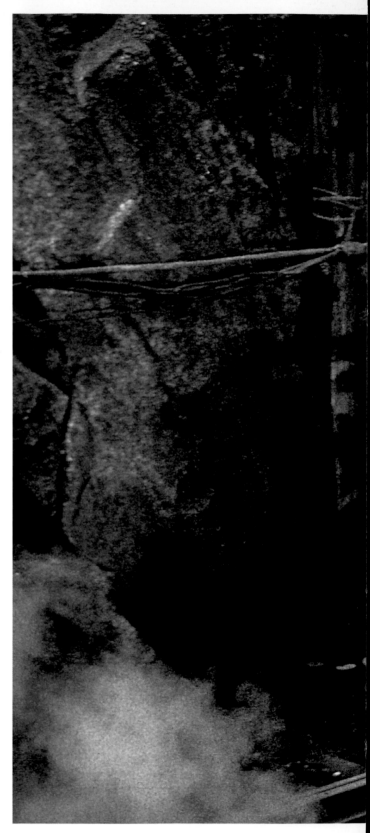

Harrison Ford, Kate Capshaw, and Ke Huy Quan in *Indiana Jones and the Temple of Doom* by Steven Spielberg (1984).

Opposite page: Sean Connery
and Harrison Ford in *Indiana
Jones and the Last Crusade*
(1989).

Above: Harrison Ford
in *Indiana Jones and
the Last Crusade* (1989).

to invent the PG-13 rating as acknowledgement of
the gray area between films made for kids and those
they should be kept away from.

By the late 1980s, Lucas was still under contract to produce two additional Indiana Jones movies for Paramount, but he was running out of ideas.
Ford wanted Indy to be an unambiguous hero. And
so *Indiana Jones and the Last Crusade* (1989) became a
family movie: Indy goes looking for his dad, who
has gone missing looking for the Holy Grail. The
film also introduced the notion of a young Indiana
Jones, played by River Phoenix. Lucas soon pacted
with ABC to produce a one-hour weekly series, *The
Young Indiana Jones Chronicles* (1992–3), with the
teenaged Indy to be played by Sean Patrick Flanery.
Taking a turn away from the grab-bag nostalgic
action adventure romps of the movies, Lucas mod-
eled the series as an educational historical drama.
"The show is much more like *Howards End* than *Raiders of the Lost Ark*," he admitted. [39] In popularity, too,
the *Chronicles* never matched the cultural phenom-
enon of the films.

(Mis)adventures in the producer's chair

Right after the release of *Indiana Jones and the Temple of Doom*, Lucas announced he would take a two-year hiatus from running Lucasfilm, the umbrella network of all of his productions and businesses. But he didn't stop working entirely: during this time Lucas used his resources and name to support pet projects for his friends and those he admired.

He first agreed to step in as executive producer on Walter Murch's directorial effort, *Return to Oz* (1985), preventing Disney from shutting down the production. He helped Paul Schrader find money for *Mishima* (1985) at Warner Brothers, and had ILM do the film's opening credits. He also helped edit *Latino* (1985), a Haskell Wexler passion project shot amidst the conflict between the Contras and the Sandinistas in Nicaragua, and helped the film find a distributor. He put money into Jim Henson's *Labyrinth* (1986), and invited his personal spiritual hero, Joseph Campbell, to use the Skywalker Ranch to shoot a TV series (*Joseph Campbell and the Power of Myth*, 1988).

Lucas tentatively stepped back into moviemaking as the producer of two disasters. *Howard the Duck*, a comic-book adaptation uneasily blending kid-friendly fantasy and bawdy adult humor, directed by Willard Huyck in 1986, went twenty percent over budget, flopped at the box office and was deemed by critics to be one of the worst movies of all time. While Lucas's postmodern approach to homage was praised by many the first few times he tried it, with *Star Wars* and *Raiders of the Lost Ark*, the same aesthetic was promptly criticized when it marked the non-franchise films he produced in the mid-1980s. *Howard the Duck*'s pastiche lacked a consistent worldview. Similarly, *Willow* (1988) was considered by many to be a hodgepodge of other better, earlier films—including Lucas's own. The story (Lucas sketched the concept, Bob Dolman was the credited screenwriter) was a blatant riff on the tales of J.R.R. Tolkien, up to and including its titular three-foot-tall, hobbit-like protagonist, played by Warwick Davis. The stew also included elements of Victor Fleming's *The Wizard of Oz* (1939), Wolfgang

Mishima by Paul Schrader (1985).

Return to Oz by Walter Murch (1985).

Reitherman's *The Sword and the Stone* (1963), Dave Fleischer's *Gulliver's Travels* (1939), and even George Miller's *Mad Max* (1979). Reviews were generally unkind; Ebert called the film "turgid and relentlessly predictable." [40]

Technology

Willow today is perhaps most notable as the production that impelled Lucas's ILM team to invent the computer graphics process known as "morphing," in which one being can be made to seamlessly transform into another. It was developed for a single shot in this forgettable film in which an actress appeared as a woman only after first passing through the bodies of a goat, ostrich, turtle, and tiger. Within three years, it would be considered the hottest advance in special effects, appearing most notably in *Terminator 2: Judgement Day* (1991) and the music video for Michael Jackson's *Black or White*.

Without directing a single film in the 1980s, George Lucas was responsible for some of the decade's most significant cinematic innovations,

fostering major advancements in film editing, computer animation and special effects technologies. Shortly after the release of *Star Wars*, Lucas had visited Coppola in the *Apocalypse Now* edit suite. Coppola had transferred the massive celluloid rushes of his shoot to video tape and wanted to show off the electronic editing suite that had been custom built so that he could edit the film himself on tape, then hand a three-quarter-inch video assembly to film editors and tell them to replicate his cut on celluloid—a herculean task, given the enormous amount of footage, the discrepancy between video time code and celluloid edge numbers, and the difference in frame rate between film (twenty-four frames per second) and video (thirty fps). Lucas wasn't impressed with Coppola's set-up. Computerized editing, he thought, had to be designed to be intuitive to editors, not computer geeks. "You want to be able to stop on a frame and move back and forth," he said. "You want to have all of the qualities of editing and everything we learned in film school about the art of editing." What Lucas wanted was a

Labyrinth by Jim Henson (1986).

Howard the Duck by Willard Huyck (1986).

George Lucas at Disneyland

In the mid-'80s, George Lucas turned down an offer to run Disney after millionaires the Bass Brothers, who Lucas had advised, took majority control of the studio. Instead, he got involved with the production of two new attractions at Disneyland. Disney CEO Michael Eisner was keen on luring teenagers to the park by building an attraction around pop superstar Michael Jackson. Lucas agreed to produce a musical film, starring Jackson and shot using new 3-D technology. Still uninterested in directing, Lucas gave his old pal Francis Ford Coppola the job. Coppola hired Rusty Lemorande to write a script, based on a concept developed in-house at Disney.

The seventeen-minute film *Captain EO* tells the story of a space traveler (Jackson) who lands on a bleak planet ruled by an evil queen (Anjelica Huston), whose cold regime is thawed by song, dance, and romance. The theater was equipped with lasers and smoke machines to further enhance the immersive nature of the 3-D film. Budgeted at $20 million, at the time of its premiere at Disneyland in 1986 *Captain EO* was the most expensive film, minute by minute, ever made. *Captain EO* played at Disneyland continuously until 1994, when it was replaced by an attraction built around the film *Honey, I Shrunk the Kids* (directed by Lucas's protégé Joe Johnson). *Captain EO* returned to the park in 2009, after Michael Jackson's death.

Something between a ride and a movie, *Star Tours* followed in 1987. Visitors to the park sat in a "ship" based on military flight simulators and watched a film meant to simulate the perspective of looking through the window of a spacecraft in flight. An unseen operator manually synced the movements of the visitor's carriage to the movements on screen. In the original attraction, the "flight," led by a pilot named Rex (voiced by Paul "Pee Wee Herman" Reubens), goes off course, gets stuck in a comet, and ends up trapped in the tractor beam of an Imperial Star Destroyer. Ultimately Rex leads the viewer into a battle replicating the destruction of the Death Star from *A New Hope*. This version of *Star Tours* ran at Disneyland until 2010, when it was replaced by a new version called *Star Tours: The Adventure Continues*. The ride now cycles randomly through fifty-four potential stories, all of them set between *The Phantom Menace* and *A New Hope* on the Star Wars timeline.

digital equivalent of a flatbed or Moviola, allowing an editor to work with sound and image together or separately, "driving" the edit while looking to a screen, and simultaneously recording data about shots and reels so the digital edit could be applied easily to cutting the physical film. Under Lucas's directive, ILM developed a software called Edit-Droid, which introduced digital archive searching and drag-and-drop usability into film editing. The software was eventually sold to AVID, and helped to define the current standard of both professional and amateur digital editing.

Digitizing the editing process was just the first step. Lucas had dreamed for years of making films in a purely digital environment—no sets, no

Left: George Lucas with Michael Jackson and Francis Ford Coppola on the set of *Captain Eo* by Francis Ford Coppola (1986).

Opposite page: *Willow* by Ron Howard (1988).

lights, no celluloid, and, to the extent possible, no actors. He felt that digital technology could free him from much of the time commitment, tedium, and hassle of the filmmaking process, and allow him more control of his productions while keeping budgets down. *The Young Indiana Jones Chronicles* TV show gave Lucas a kind of sandbox in which to experiment with generating sets and actors digitally, at a fraction on the cost of shooting practicals and living people. In 1994, Lucas named Martin Scorsese's *The Age of Innocence* (1993) as an example of a kind of movie that only the upper echelon of filmmakers could find money to mount. Lucas claimed he had found a better way. "On the *Young Indy* series—which is also a period show with horses, carriages, completely different landscapes, costumes—we had exactly the same kinds of production values as Age of Innocence, but we did it for 10% of the cost, thanks to digital technology. We used the computer to make crowd scenes, when we only had a handful of actors, and to replicate backgrounds that weren't really there. We did a shot in the TV series for $1500 that would have cost a studio $30,000 if they were doing the same shot for a feature film."[41]

The 1994 film *Radioland Murders*—based on an old Lucas concept, it was directed by Mel Smith—was producer Lucas's experiment in bringing the low-cost, highly innovative methods developed for the *Young Indy* TV series into the production of a feature film. A period comedy—mystery budgeted at a relatively low $15 million, *Radioland* had more than 100 effects shots—a huge amount for that time. Shot in North Carolina, the set was linked fiber optically to Lucasfilm's base camp in Northern California. Lucas checked in on the set via video feed in the mornings, from home. "I'm a writer-director-editor-producer, I'm very much more comfortable working in the medium the way a painter or sculptor or somebody would," Lucas said at a press conference that year. "You basically put on a layer, then put on another layer, then you step back and look at it and put on another layer. And that's what we've been doing in the filmmaking process."[42] In 1991, *Heir to the Empire*, a Star Wars spin-off novel written by Timothy Zahn with Lucas's blessing, topped the *New York Times* bestseller list. Sales of Star Wars toys and merchandise started to climb again, certainly not hurt by Fox's 1993 release of the remastered

trilogy on home video. These successes combined to plant the seed in Lucas's mind that maybe the time was right to return to the universe and mythology he had left behind. Meanwhile, Lucas made an effort to repair the bridges to Hollywood that he had burned a decade earlier. Receptive to playing a role in his redemption, the Academy of Motion Picture Arts and Sciences gave Lucas their honorary Irving Thallberg Award in 1992.

While all of these activities prepared Lucas in some way for his return to directing, the most momentous project he was involved with in the decade and a half between the original release of *Return of the Jedi* and the theatrical release of the special editions may have been a film on which he himself wasn't credited. The computer-generated dinosaurs in Steven Spielberg's *Jurassic Park*, created by ILM, broke massive new ground for creature effects in Hollywood. Lucas was not shy about his company's accomplishment. "We did a test for Steven Spielberg," Lucas remembered in 1994, "And when we put them up on the screen, I had tears in my eyes. It was like one of those moments in history, like the invention of the light bulb or the first telephone call. A major gap had been crossed, and things were never going to be the same."[43] Lucas was inspired by the achievement, but he was also, as ever, competitive. If such groundbreaking work was going to be done by his company, he wanted to get authorial credit. And when *Jurassic Park*'s domestic gross of $357 million edged past *Star Wars*' $322 million at the top of the all-time chart, he had a financial bragging rights incentive, too. By 1995, *Variety* confirmed that George Lucas was writing three new Star Wars films, to go into production by the end of the millennium.

Jurassic Park
by Steven Spielberg (1993).

The second trilogy

The Phantom Menace, Attack of the Clones, and *Revenge of the Sith*

Ray Park in *The Phantom Menace* (1999).

Since first discovering experimental film in his teens, George Lucas had longed to pursue a painterly approach to cinema. By the mid-1990s, technology had caught up with Lucas's vision. It would now be possible to tinker with his previous films, with the ease and autonomy of a painter touching up a canvas. And new films could be created in an almost entirely digital environment.

Persecuted victims

Confident in the viability of new digital working methods based on the *Radioland Murders* experience, Lucas set out to test the market viability of a return to the Star Wars franchise, through the Special Editions re-releases of the trilogy, which hit North American theaters in early 1997. The original Star Wars films pushed model animation, practical special effects, and computer-controlled photography about as far as they would be pushed before the advent of the digital era. They were also relatively low-cost productions, carefully framed and edited to make the most of thinly stretched budgets. Lucas pitched the Special Edition re-releases as an opportunity to use new technology to realize a vision that had been compromised by the limitations of the first trilogy's production. "It is what

it was meant to be originally," he said of the new versions. "We just didn't have the wherewithal to do it then."[44]

Essentially, three types of changes were made. Cosmetic restorations of sound and picture quality cleaned up errors (particularly in continuity and color timing) and replaced archaic effects with updated versions. Lucas also added scenes and characters, to restore aspects of the story and the setting that were in his original scripts but had to be dropped during production or post-production largely due to budget constraints. Finally, and most controversially, Lucas made a few seemingly minor changes that were taken by fans as revisions of basic tenets of the Star Wars mythology.

Some of the cosmetic adjustments were virtually undetectable to the naked eye. In the final victory celebration sequence of *A New Hope* (reminiscent of *Triumph of the Will*, a 1935 Nazi propaganda film by Leni Riefenstahl), human extras were composited in to replace what had been cardboard cutouts in the original film. Other changes were visually noticeable, if not narratively significant. In *A New Hope*, for instance, the explosion of the Death Star was digitally redone, and new characters (digital alien extras, really) were added to the film's

Mos Eisley cantina sequence. The Cloud City in *The Empire Strikes Back* was infused with additional, digital clouds, and a full musical number was added to the scene set in Jabba's lair in *Return of the Jedi*.

Other changes, however, arguably altered the original story. Throughout the Special Edition of *Star Wars Episode IV: A New Hope*, Lucas made small digital tweaks in fight scenes to amplify the firepower directed at the heroes and to minimize their use of weapons against the bad guys. A lot of these additions and subtractions happened in scenes that move so quickly, individually, they might go unnoticed. But added together, the overall effect was to remake the heroes from the Rebels they were into persecuted victims.

The fan outrage was not enough to prevent the Special Editions from making big money at the box office. Having cost roughly $11 million to produce in 1977 and another $10 million to restore, the new *A New Hope* grossed $36.2 million in the first weekend of its re-release alone. The film added $138 million to its US box-office receipts, easily surpassing *Jurassic Park* and becoming the highest grossing film of all time at the US box office (it was soon toppled from that perch by *Titanic*). The re-releases of *The Empire Strikes Back* and *Return of the Jedi* also did well, although they did not come close to matching *A New Hope*'s staggering numbers. "The success of that rerelease not only told me that I could create these creatures and build better sets and towns than I could before, but that the Star Wars audience was still alive—it hadn't completely disappeared after 15 years," Lucas told *Wired* magazine. "I decided that if I didn't do the backstory then, I never would."[45]

A hole in the market

Lucas warned as early as 1981 that the prequels would feel different. "The first trilogy will not be as much of an action adventure kind of thing. Maybe we'll make it have some humor, but right now it's much more humorless than this one. This one is where all the excitement is, which is why I started

Han shot first

When the first of the Star Wars trilogy, *A New Hope*, was re-released in 1997, the alteration that most troubled the Star Wars faithful was that of the cantina scene. In the original version of the scene, in the meeting between Han Solo and the alien thug Greedo, Han, sensing that Greedo was about to fire his blaster at point-blank range, beat his enemy to the punch by firing his own gun. In the Special Edition, the scene was re-edited and digitally altered so that Greedo shoots first and misses Han. Only then does Lucas's anti-hero fire his own blaster to blow his enemy away. This change enraged fans in 1997, and continues to be a controversial topic, with some proclaiming that Han's short temper and quick reaction to a perceived threat is crucial to the conception of the character as a selfish bastard who, over the course of the film, learns how to care about other people and eventually becomes a hero.

The phrase "Han Shoots First" has become an undying internet meme and T-shirt slogan, thanks in part to a petition circulated on the website, HanShootsFirst.org, which referred to the edit as "a crime." In 2004, Lucas firmly defended the new version of the scene, which he insisted wasn't a narrative change but a clarification. "The way it got cobbled together at the time, it came off that [Han] fired first. He didn't fire first," Lucas said. He explained that, when making the film, he didn't get a shot he needed and tried to "fudge it editorially. In my mind [Greedo] shot first or at the same time." Lucas went on to make a pointed judgment of fans who held the original version dear. "We like to think of [Han Solo] as a murderer because that's hip—I don't think that's a good thing for people. I mean, I don't see how you could redeem somebody who kills people in cold blood." Lucas seemed to soften on that stance over time.

In 2006, the original version of the film was released on DVD alongside the altered version, and in 2007, on the set of *Indiana Jones and the Kingdom of the Crystal Skull*, Lucas was photographed wearing a "Han Shoots First" t-shirt.

Opposite page:
Top left: *Star Wars* (1977), 1997 re-release.
Top right: *The Empire Strikes Back* (1980), 1997 re-release.
Bottom: Harrison Ford in *Star Wars* (1977), 1997 re-release.

Right: George Lucas with Harrison Ford on the set of *Indiana Jones and the Kingdom of the Crystal Skull* by Steven Spielberg (2008).

with it. The other ones are a little more Machiavellian. It's all plotting—more of a mystery."[46] Lucas's decision to direct the prequels himself seemed to come to pass because it was the best way for him to have complete control as a producer. "If I were to [make the prequels] the way I'd done the other Star Wars films, they would be astronomically expensive," he said.[47]

Though positioned as the first cinematic chapter of the Star Wars saga, *Star Wars Episode I: The Phantom Menace* still begins with the *de rigueur* crawl, setting the scene via backstory. The trade federation has levied an embargo on the tiny planet of Naboo. Two ambassadors from the Jedi council have been sent to find a diplomatic solution to the matter, but instead of a negotiation, Qui-Gon Jinn

Liam Neeson, Kenny Baker, Jake Lloyd, and Ewan McGregor in *The Phantom Menace* (1999).

Opposite page: Liam Neeson, Ray Park, and Ewan McGregor in *The Phantom Menace* (1999).

Following pages: Jake Lloyd, Khan Bonfils, Silas Carson and Samuel L. Jackson in *The Phantom Menace* (1999).

(Liam Neeson) and Obi-Wan Kenobi (Ewan McGregor) find a fight. The evil Darth Sidious—an alter ego of the future Emperor Palpatine, played here, as in *The Return of the Jedi*, by Ian McDiarmid—has ordered his army to kill them. Unprepared for an ambush, the Jedis flee. Regrouping in Naboo's woods, they meet Jar Jar Binks, a Gungan who speaks in a squeaky, cre-ole-meets-baby-talk patois sprinkled with would-be catchphrases ("Ex-squeeze me!"). Jar Jar accompanies the Jedi on their quest to free Naboo's Queen Ami-dala, who has been imprisoned by the Federation.

   The Jedis successfully free the Queen, but their getaway ship is damaged by gunfire, forc-ing the group, which has brought along Amidala's handmaiden Padme (Natalie Portman), to land on the planet of Tattoine for repairs. There they meet Anakin Skywalker (Jake Lloyd), a young slave boy and amateur mechanic who immediately takes a liking to Padme. The Jedis sense that the Force is strong in Anakin, and wonder if he could be the "chosen one" as foretold in a prophecy. There's a pod race coming up in the town, and the Jedis make a deal that if Anakin wins the race, his owner will release him into their custody. He does win, and travels with the crew back to Naboo, where it is revealed that Padme is actually Queen Amidala, and the woman posing as the Queen (played by Kiera Knightley) was merely a decoy to protect her. Qui-Gonn wants to train Anakin as a Jedi, but Yoda (played in this film by new puppets, again voiced by Frank Oz) is concerned that the boy is too attached to his mother and that his future is "clouded by fear." 79

But soon, Qui-Gon is killed, and Obi-Wan agrees to honor his dying wish that Anakin become Obi-Wan's apprentice. As *The Phantom Menace* ends, the stage is set for Anakin to grow into Obi-Wan's Jedi equal and Padme's love interest, and for Palpatine/ Sidious to continue to play the Republic from both sides in pursuit of world domination.

What is the Phantom Menace? Is it the two-faced Palpatine, who fronts as a friend to our heroes while secretly acting in league with their enemies? Or is it Anakin, the apparently immaculately conceived child who seems as sweet and guileless as can be, but nonetheless sets off Yoda and Obi-wan's trouble sensors? The title is perhaps the only ambiguity of the movie. Lucas is intentionally speaking to a young audience—even younger than the teenagers he was aiming for with the original films—and much of *Phantom Menace* is thus suitably pandering. Arguably, once again there was a hole in the

market that needed to be filled; consider the earnest squareness of *The Phantom Menace* in relation to the other big sci-fi blockbuster of 1999, Wachowski brothers' *The Matrix*.

Film critic J. Hoberman called *The Phantom Menace* "the most anticipated movie in living memory."[48] For many critics, the end result did not justify the wait. Some bashed Lucas's blinkered worldview, embodied by alien characters whose apparent ethnic stereotypes could not be ignored. Wrote Charles Taylor on Salon.com, "Lucas miscalculates badly with the new creature, Jar-Jar Binks, which, with its quasi-Caribbean dialect and jivey carriage, strays uncomfortably into the realm of racial caricature, though a bigger problem is that most of his dialogue is almost totally unintelligible."[49] Even critics who generally approved of the film tended to cite such characterizations as problematic. "Lucas's first instalment sustains the gee-whiz spirit of the series and offers a swashbuckling extragalactic getaway, creating illusions that are even more plausible than the kitchen-raiding raptors of *Jurassic Park*," wrote Janet Maslin in the *New York Times*. "[But] the filmmakers could have been smarter about throwaway references when it came to the ethnic hallmarks of their creatures. Some of the most unsightly villains sound embarrassingly like Hollywood's old stereotypes from the mysterious Orient."[50] *The Phantom Menace*, indeed, feels like a movie made by an artist drunk on the possibilities of technology and tone deaf to the culture. The digital environments are beautiful, but the characters are hollow. The fully digital creatures, in particular, lack the weight, literally and figuratively, of characters formerly played by puppets (such as Jabba the Hutt) or men in suits (C-3PO, whose spare-parts construction chronicled in *The Phantom Menace*—even though the character is fully digitally animated).

In responding to criticism of the prequels, Lucas again chided audiences for their bloodlust. "People expected *Episode III*, which is where Anakin turns into Darth Vader, to be *Episode I*. And then they expected *Episodes II* and *III* to be Darth Vader going around cutting people's heads off and terrorizing the universe. But how did he get to be Darth Vader? You have to explore him in relationships, and you have to see where he started. He was a sweet kid, helpful, just like most people imagine

Opposite page: Natalie Portman in *The Phantom Menace* (1999).

The Phantom Menace (1999).

83

themselves to be. Most people said, 'This guy must have been a horrible little brat—a demon child.' But the point is, he wasn't born that way—he became that way and thought he was doing the right thing. He eventually realizes he's going down the dark path, but he thinks it's justifiable. The idea is to see how a democracy becomes a dictatorship, and how a good person goes bad—and still, in the end, thinks he's doing the right thing." [51]

A stunning mise-en-scène

However, although the presence of Jar Jar and other noxious new characters was lessened in *Episode II: Attack of the Clones* (2002) and *Episode III: Revenge of the Sith* (2005), these remaining prequels had their own problems.

Attack of the Clones catches up with Anakin (now played by the pretty but wooden Hayden Christiansen) ten years into his Jedi training. A separatist movement (the bad guys) has been mobilized by Count Dooku (Christopher Lee) against the Galactic Republic (the good guys), and an assassination attempt has been made on Padme Amidala (played again by Portman), who is now a senator. Chancellor Palpatine—whose secret identity as Darth Sidious is still unknown to our heroes—assigns Anakin and Obi-Wan to protect Amidala. The film splits into two, interwoven stories. Obi-Wan, investigating the

Ewan McGregor and Temuera Morrison in *Attack of the Clones* (2002).

threat on Padme's life, goes on a journey to the planet of Kamino and discovers that someone has ordered the development of an army of clone soldiers. Meanwhile, on Padme's home planet of Naboo, the senator and her bodyguard, Anakin, fall in love. In the final scene, Anakin and Padme secretly marry. The film ends with the newly married couple kissing. He smiles, and she looks terrified.

At a running time of 142 minutes, *Attack of the Clones* is the longest of the three prequel films, and with its preponderance of plot, hokey romance dialogue, impenetrable political dialogue, and sometimes unintelligible action sequences (a third-act chase through the clone factory is particularly

difficult to parse), its length feels interminable. But of the three prequels, *Attack of the Clones* also has the most by which to recommend it. The first feature film to be shot on the high-definition digital format 24p, *Attack of the Clones* is, aesthetically, an excellent argument for the format. Shifting back and forth between dystopian cities, the lushly verdant paradise backdrop of Anakin and Padme's courtship, and over-the-top civil-war battles as barbaric as they are high-tech, Lucas's synthetic *mise-en-scène* is never less than stunning. An early flying car chase is all lush washes of neon color; a fight in an asteroid field creates an incredible sense depth—almost more three-dimensional than 3-D. *Attack of the Clones*

Hayden Christensen and Natalie Portman in *Attack of the Clones* (2002).

Following pages: Ewan McGregor in *Attack of the Clones* (2002).

is also where Lucas's pains to create synchronicity between the two trilogies feels the most purposeful. The film sets up a dynamic tension between Anakin and Obi-Wan similar to that between Luke and Han, but somewhat less brotherly. Like the other middle movie, *The Empire Strikes Back*, it sets our two main male heroes on separate journeys, resolving in uncertainty—and the Skywalker male losing a limb.

The end of an exhausting series

In the final Star Wars film, *Episode III: Revenge of the Sith*, Anakin Skywalker is finally transformed into Darth Vader. At the start of the protracted narrative (the film is almost as long as *Attack of the Clones* at 140 minutes, and even more turgid in its pacing), Anakin executes the previous film's elusive antagonist, Count Dooku—but the Jedis have still

not figured out that the real threat is Chancellor Palpatine, head of the Republic, or that he is also the evil Darth Sidious. The film charts Palpatine's seduction of Anakin, which leads the still wide-eyed young Jedi to sell out his ideals in the hopes of protecting his newly pregnant wife Padme. The battle for Anakin's soul comes down to the piece-meal destruction of his body: in a lightsaber duel, Obi-Wan dismembers his former protégé's legs and remaining arm, leaving him to be immolated by lava. The film ends with Padme dying in childbirth (her twins, Luke and Leia, are separated), Obi-Wan and Yoda going off on separate exiles, and Palpatine rebuilding what's left of Anakin's horribly burned body with cybernetic limbs. When Anakin learns Padme has died, he tilts his head to the sky and bellows a dramatic cry: "Noooo!" With nothing good

left to live for, he submits fully to the Dark Side, the transformation into Darth Vader complete.

Revenge of the Sith was fairly well reviewed. Many American critics, as if relieved that the exhausting series was coming to an end, looked past the film's own merits and demerits and used their review as an opportunity to consider—and commend, if with reservations—Lucas's accomplishments across six films. "George Lucas has achieved what few artists do; he has created and populated a world of his own," wrote Roger Ebert. "*Revenge of the Sith* is a great entertainment."[52] *The New Yorker*'s Anthony Lane famously offered a dissenting voice. "What Lucas has devised, over six movies, is a terrible puritan dream: a morality tale in which both sides are bent on moral cleansing, and where their differences can be assuaged only by a triumphant circus of violence," he wrote. Lane

Film preservation

In 1988, George Lucas joined Steven Spielberg and other filmmakers in an appearance before the United States Congress, in defense of an artist's right to keep their work from being altered against their consent. "Today, engineers with their computers can add color to black-and-white movies, change the soundtrack, speed up the pace, and add or subtract material to the philosophical tastes of the copyright holder," Lucas told Congress. "Tomorrow, more advanced technology will be able to replace actors with "fresher faces," or alter dialogue and change the movement of the actor's lips to match. It will soon be possible to create a new "original" negative with whatever changes or alterations the copyright holder of the moment desires ... In the future it will become even easier for old negatives to become lost and be 'replaced' by new altered negatives. This would be a great loss to our society. Our cultural history must not be allowed to be rewritten." (United States Congress, 1988) And yet, with each subsequent release of new versions of the Star Wars films, Lucas takes a step toward making his original versions of the movies obsolete. "The other versions will disappear," Lucas confirmed in 1997. "Even the 35 million [VHS] tapes of Star Wars out there won't last more than 30 or 40 years. A hundred years from now, the only version of the movie that anyone will remember will be the DVD version ... I think it's the director's prerogative, not the studio's to go back and reinvent a movie."

In 2004, Lucas further defended his digital reinvention of his movies by comparing the advancements in cinema technology to a similar evolution in fine art, when oil painting replaced frescoes. "[Oil paintings] could be made by a much smaller group of people, or even by an individual. And most importantly, the medium gave an artist great creative flexibility—he could change his mind, work the painting, repaint areas over and over, and get a kind of malleability he simply didn't have with frescoes."

Hayden Christensen and Ewan McGregor in *Revenge of the Sith* (2005).

conceded that his skepticism was unusual. "Judging from the whoops and crowings that greeted the opening credits, this is the only dream we are good for. We get the films we deserve." [53]

"Noooo!"

The generation that constituted Star Wars' most fervent fan base were school-aged in the late '70s and early '80s, and by the turn of the millennium, this generation had become the primary drivers of internet culture. In their hands, the prequels were scrutinized in the time of their theatrical release in ways in which the films of the original trilogy could never have been. The boom in social networking coincided with the release of *Revenge of the Sith*, spawning millions of blog posts, videos, comments, and articles in a still-running, constantly self-propagating conversation.

Of the massive amount of Star Wars arcana on the internet, the continuing stickiness of one bit taken directly from the final prequel seems particularly significant. A five-second clip of Darth Vader's cry of "Noooo!" in the final moments of *Revenge of the Sith* circulated around the web and soon became the basis for countless parody videos. As a meme, it underscored what many fans felt was the core disappointment of the prequels. That Lucas chose to express his protagonist-turned-antagonist's unfathomable pain and self-hatred by putting such an unoriginal cry in his mouth was indicative of how far Lucas himself had traveled, from an innovator and rule-breaker serving a personal vision to the embodiment of stale cliché. The "Vader Nooo!", according to blogger Darrin Franich, was "the precise moment when Darth Vader stopped being one of the great villains in cinema history and started being a punchline." [54]

In favor of the camera

Even from an objective standpoint, the prequels differ from the original films in a few key ways that don't flatter the more recently made films. First and foremost, the screenplays seem to suffer from a lack of collaboration. While Lucas sought counsel from friends on the *Star Wars* script, and outsourced entirely the writing of the screenplays for *The Empire Strikes Back* and *Return of the Jedi*, he wrote *The Phantom Menace* and *Revenge of the Sith* alone (Jonathan Hales, a veteran of the *Young Indiana Jones* TV series, pitched in on *Attack of the Clones*). Where the original three films were marked by banter, particularly between Han and Leia and Han and Luke, the dialogue in the prequels amounts to either stone-faced exposition (such as the moment in *The Phantom Menace* when Anakin asks Qui-Gon to explain the concept of midi-chlorians, the blood organisms that,

Revenge of the Sith (2005)

Opposite page: Natalie Portman and Hayden Christensen in *Revenge of the Sith* (2005).

according to the film, measure one's sensitivity to the Force) or are unnaturally stilted. The romantic scenes between Anakin and Padme in *Attack of the Clones* and *Revenge of the Sith* are particularly risible. Lucas, who in his twenties made one of the best films about teenage courtship rituals of all time in *American Graffiti*, had by late middle-age apparently forgotten how humans, let alone young lovers, speak to one another. The rare wisecracks in these movies are stale and unfunny, the performances uncommonly flat.

The prequels are also considerably weighed down by their bloat. Freed from budgetary constraints, able to produce virtually anything he can imagine digitally, Lucas often allows battle and action scenes to go on forever, padding them out with sweeping wide shots full of synthetic characters and vehicles in conflict. The higher the ratio of computer-generated imagery to "real" humans and objects in the prequels, the more distanced the films feel from basic real-world consequences. Perhaps this owes to the lack of visible human bloodshed in the later Wars. Is it a coincidence that most of the prequels' "victims" at the hands of our heroes are either non-living (droids, clones) or contained within ships, and thus unseen?

In 1974, Lucas admitted that in his first film, *THX 1138*, "Some of the dramatic was sacrificed in favor of the camera."[55] This ends up being a succinct

and accurate assessment of what works and what doesn't work in the prequels. They are beautifully designed films, but they're also dramatically inert and often painfully written. At the start of his career, Lucas was aware that writing was the weakest of his talents. "I don't have a natural talent for writing," he admitted in 1974. "When I sit down and bleed on the page, it's just awful." Back then, he had the self-awareness to bring in other writers to stop the bleeding, to take his seeds of ideas and shape them into something fit for consumption. The prequels are, for better and for worse, pure Lucas. They were built so independently that there was no one to tell him "no." Even former collaborators were disappointed. The prequels, Walter Murch told *Wired*, "pummel you into submission. You say, OK, OK, there are 20,000 robots walking across the field. If you told me a 14-year-old had done them on his home computer, I would get very excited, but if you tell me it's George Lucas—with all of the resources available to him—I know it's amazing, but I don't feel it's amazing."[56]

Despite the criticism the prequels have inspired, they were still financially successful. Propelled by fifteen years worth of anticipation, *The Phantom Menace* made $430 million, and became one of the top ten highest grossing films of all time at the US box office. The other prequels were comparatively commercially unremarkable. *Attack of* the Clones made $310 million dollars—just barely clearing the $309 million total of *Return of the Jedi,* which, if adjusted for inflation, would be more like $667 million today. *Revenge of the Sith* topped out at $380 million—good, but not great for the closing film of what was then the biggest franchise of all time. It was recently surpassed at the domestic box office by the final film in the Harry Potter franchise.

Revisions

The difference between Star Wars and other franchises, of course, is that Lucas cannot seem to leave his ostensibly completed series alone. He altered the films yet again for DVD releases in 2004 and Blu-Ray releases in 2011. The most significant changes to the 2004 version involved the digital insertion of actors from the prequel films. Ian McDiarmid, who

played Emperor Palpatine in Episodes I—III and VI, was inserted into a hologram image in conversation with Vader in *The Empire Strikes Back*. A few lines of dialogue were added to the scene; in one, Palpatine tells Vader that "the offspring of Anakin Skywalker" is a threat to them. At the very end of the original *Return of the Jedi*, Luke saw spectral versions of Obi-Wan, Yoda, and Anakin Skywalker—Luke's father, free of the trappings of Darth Vader in the afterlife—looking happily on the proceedings. In the 2004 version, Lucas replaced the actor who played Anakin in Jedi, Sebastian Shaw, with Hayden Christiansen, who played the young Anakin in the prequels.

All six films were released on Blu-Ray in 2011 with yet more changes. The two most talked about alterations came at either end of the series. In *The Phantom Menace*, Lucas replaced the Frank Oz-puppeted Yoda

Ray Winstone, Shia LaBeouf and Harrison Ford in Steven Spielberg's *Indiana Jones and the Kingdom of the Crystal Skull* (2008).

with a digital version, to create consistency with the CGI Yoda in the following two films. And, in the climactic scene of *Return of the Jedi* when the Emperor uses "Force lightning" to electrocute Luke and Vader steps in to save his son, killing the Emperor and himself in the process, Vader's formerly silent self-sacrifice has now been dubbed with a dramatic cry of "No! Noooo!" This echoes the cry made by Christensen's Anakin at the end of *Revenge of the Sith*. Fan reaction to these changes was, predictably, negative. "Lucas is so out of touch," wrote blogger Devin Faraci. "And [he] loves the idea of on the nose symmetry between the two trilogies." [57]

How out of touch is he? Lucas has long been accused of instigating a change in industry standards, a newfound prioritizing of quick-grossing blockbusters over quality adult cinema. But he has refused to admit responsibility for initiating a shift in viewing habits away from serious films. On the contrary, he has often protested that his highly successful films allowed more "quality adult cinema" to be seen. "You need movies that make a lot of money in order to finance the ones that don't make money," he said in the late 1990s. "Of the billion and a half dollars that *Star Wars* made, half of it went to theater owners. And what did the theater owners do with that? They built multiplexes. Once they had all these screens, they had to book them with something, which meant that the art films that were being shown in tiny places in the middle of nowhere, suddenly were playing in mainstream cinemas, and started making money ... So in a way, I did destroy the Hollywood film industry, only I destroyed it by making films more intelligent, not by making films infantile." [58]

Life after Star Wars and Indy?

Once the prequels were in the can, Lucas insisted it was time for him to take the turn toward the avant-garde that he had long threatened. "I've earned the right to fail," he said in 2004, "Which means making what I think are really great movies that no one wants to see." [59] But those movies have not yet been seen by anyone. Instead, Lucas delved into the fourth Indiana Jones film, the much-maligned *Indiana Jones and the Kingdom of the Crystal Skull* (2008). The year 2012 brought the release of the Lucas-financed *Red Tails* (Anthony Hemingway, 2012), a big-budget, heavily digitized action period piece about the first squadron of African–American military fighter pilots, which

Lucas has been talking about making since the first Star Wars trilogy was in production. A month after *Red Tails* hit US theaters, so did another Lucasfilm production: the re-release of *The Phantom Menace*, in 3-D; 3-D versions of the other films in the franchise were expected to follow.

You could call Lucas's constant tinkering with the two blockbusters that made his name and fortune the nerd equivalent of a man in midlife crisis getting plastic surgery and buying a sports car—terrified of irrelevance, he obsessively remakes his legacy. But the oft-cited flaws of the prequels—particularly the coldness of the characterizations within stories bogged down with impenetrable language and detail—make them fascinating as continuations of the quasi-autobiography of the original Star Wars trilogy. After spending a decade alone in a compound, building a

Hayden Christensen
in *Revenge of the Sith* (2005).

(business) empire that kept him abreast of technology but removed from people, Lucas made a series of movies about trade federations and interplanetary politics that lacked the pulse of contemporary human life. The films' inability to understand people is reflective of Lucas's own personal history. Lucas's experimental filmmaking ambitions may have remained unrealized, but a more sympathetic read suggests that for Lucas, as for Vader, this was not a choice at all: instead, he has become trapped by his own creation, a rebel whose phenomenal success turned him, unwillingly, into an impenetrable power.

"I'm not happy that corporations have taken over the film industry, but now I find myself being the head of a corporation, so there's a certain irony there," Lucas declared in 2004. "I have become the very thing that I was trying to avoid. That is Darth Vader."[60] 97

Chronology

1944

May 14. George Lucas, Jr is born in Modesto, CA.

1958–62

As a teenager, Lucas becomes obsessed with building, fixing, and racing cars. His experience of "cruising" the main drag of Modesto inspired *American Graffiti*.

1962

Days before his high school graduation, Lucas nearly dies in a car crash. He emerges from the hospital scared straight, abandons dreams of a career in cars, and enrolls in Modesto Junior College.

1964

Develops friendship with Haskell Wexler and moves to Los Angeles to enroll in film school at the University of Southern California (USC).

1965

Makes first short films, *Freiheit* and *Look at Life*.

1967

Goes to work as an assistant for editor Verna Fields on a documentary about President Johnson for the United States Information Agency. Meets and starts dating Marcia Griffin, a more advanced editor on the project. Shoots an experimental short on the set of J. Lee Thompson's *Mackenna's Gold*. Begins a six-month internship at Warner Brothers, working on the set of *Finian's Rainbow*, and befriends its director, Francis Ford Coppola. Meets Steven Spielberg. Completes *Electronic Labyrinth THX 1138 4EB* as a graduate student short.

1968

Serves as Coppola's right-hand man on the set of *The Rain People*, while making the behind-the-scenes documentary *Filmmaker*. Starts writing feature-length adaptation of the *THX* short.

1969

February 22. Marries Marcia Griffin. With Coppola, co-founds independent studio American Zoetrope in San Francisco. **September.** Begins filming feature version of *THX 1138*.

1970

Disastrous screening of *THX 1138* for Warner Brothers executives leads to the studio recutting the film.

1971

March 11. *THX 1138* is released, and bombs at the box office. Creation of Lucasfilm Limited.

1972

June. *American Graffiti* begins production in Petaluma, California.

1973

American Graffiti opens, and grosses $55 million worldwide.

1974

American Graffiti is nominated for five Oscars. Lucas gets two nominations, for Best Screenplay and Best Director. Starts writing *Star Wars*.

1975

Begins assembling an effects crew, led by John Dykstra, to work on *Star Wars*. Lucas brands the team Industrial Light and Magic.

1976

Begins shooting *Star Wars*.

1977

May 25. *Star Wars* opens in theaters. It's a massive success, finishing its initial theatrical run as the highest grossing film of all time.

1978

Nominated for ten Oscars, *Star Wars* loses Best Picture, Best Director, and Best Screenplay to *Annie Hall* and Woody Allen, but the film wins six prizes. Marcia Lucas goes home with a trophy (for Best Editing); George Lucas does not. *American Graffiti* is re-released and takes in an additional $68 million. Marcia and George Lucas purchase the land on which they'll build Skywalker Ranch.

1980

May 21. *The Empire Strikes Back* opens. Lucas quits the Writers Guild (WGA) and Director's Guild (DGA) over a dispute regarding the film's lack of opening credits.

1981

June 21. *Raiders of the Lost Ark* is released. George and Marcia adopt their first child, Amanda. *Star Wars* is re-released theatrically for the first time, retitled *Star Wars Episode IV: A New Hope*.

1982

George and Marcia Lucas announce their intention to divorce.

1983

May 25. *Return of the Jedi* is released.

George Lucas (center) on the set of *6-18-67* (1967).

George Lucas with Maggie McOmie and Robert Duvall on the set of *THX 1138* (1971).

George Lucas on the set of *Star Wars* (1977).

John Dykstra on the set of *Star Wars* (1977).

1984

May 23. *Indiana Jones and the Temple of Doom* is released. **May.** Lucas takes a two-year hiatus from management of Lucasfilm.

1986

August 1. *Howard the Duck* is released and is a notable disaster. **September 13.** *Captain EO* debuts at Disneyland in Southern California. The 3-D short film, directed by Coppola and starring Michael Jackson and Anjelica Huston, is written and produced by Lucas.

1987

Star Tours, a ride-film hybrid set in the Star Wars universe, debuts at Disneyland.

1988

George Lucas appears before US Congress to speak about the importance of copyholders' rights and film preservation. **May 20.** *Willow* is released.

1989

May 24. *Indiana Jones and the Last Crusade* is released. *Star Wars* is on the first slate of films included in the National Film Registry of the US Library of Congress.

1991

Star Wars spin-off novel *Heir to the Empire* hits the New York Times bestseller list.

1992

Lucas is given the Irving Thalberg honorary award at the Academy Awards; quietly rejoins WGA and DGA. **March 4.** *The Young Indiana Jones Chronicles* is first broadcast on US television.

1993

June 11. *Jurassic Park* is released. The sophistication of its ILM-created effects, combined with its massive box-office success, which threaten the record set by *Star Wars*, help propel Lucas to move forward with the Special Editions and prequels.

1994

October 21. *Radioland Murders* is released.

1995

Lucas starts writing Star Wars prequels. *American Graffiti* is inducted into the National Film Registry of the US Library of Congress.

1996

The first official Star Wars website is launched.

1997

Lucas returns to directing: production begins on *Star Wars Episode I: The Phantom Menace.* The Special Edition re-releases of the Star Wars trilogy begin.

1999

Star Wars Episode I: The Phantom Menace is released in North American theaters.

2002

Star Wars Episode II: Attack of the Clones is released in North American theaters.

2004

Lucas releases the original Star Wars trilogy on DVD, with a host of new digital changes.

2005

Star Wars Episode III: Revenge of the Sith is released in North American theaters.

2006

The unaltered original versions of the Star Wars films are made available on DVD for the first time.

2008

Indiana Jones and the Kingdom of the Crystal Skull premieres at the Cannes Film Festival.

2011

All six Star Wars films are released on Blu-ray, with yet more alterations supervised by Lucas.

2012

Red Tails, produced by George Lucas and directed by Anthony Hemingway, is released theatrically. The 3-D restoration of *The Phantom Menace* is released in North American theaters.

George Lucas with Michael Jackson and Francis Ford Coppola on the set of *Captain Eo* by Francis Ford Coppola (1986).

George Lucas with Kate Capshaw, Steven Spielberg, and Harrison Ford on the set of *Indiana Jones and the Temple of Doom* (1984).

Jurassic Park by Steven Spielberg (1993).

George Lucas with Anthony Daniels on the set of *Attack of the Clones* (2002).

Harrison Ford in *Indiana Jones and the Kingdom of the Crystal Skull* by Steven Spielberg (2008).

Filmography

SHORT FILMS

Look at Life 1965
Format 16mm. **Running time** 1 min.
• A photomontage of notable news-media images from the year of 1965. Completed as an assignment for an animation course at the University of Southern California.

Herbie 1966
Format 16mm. **Co-Director** Paul Golding. **Running time** 3 mins.
• An experimental short consisting of abstract images of light captured in traffic at night, scored to music by Herbie Hancock.

Freiheit 1966
Format 16mm. **Running time** 3 mins. With Randal Kleiser.
• A student is shot trying to run across the Berlin border. As he lies dying, he thinks about freedom.

1:42.08
A Man and His Car 1966
Format 16mm. **Running time** 7 mins, 30 secs.
• A documentary short featuring Peter Brock driving his Lotus 23 race car on a circular track at full speed. He completes the lap in one minute, forty-two seconds.

The Emperor 1967
Format 16mm. **Running time** 24 mins. With Bob Hudson.
• A short documentary about radio DJ Bob Hudson.

Electronic Labyrinth
THX 1138 4EB 1967
Format 16mm. **Running time** 15 mins. With Dan Natchsheim and Joy Carmichael.
• A Big Brother-like government uses computers and surveillance technology in an attempt to keep one of their citizens from making an escape.

Anyone Lived
in a Pretty How Town 1967
Format 16mm. **Running time** 6 mins. With John Strawbridge, Nancy Yates, and Lance Larson.
• An adaptation of the e.e. cummings poem about life in a small town.

6-18-67 1967
Format 16mm. **Running time** 4 mins.
• A documentary short about the beauty of the desert, shot on the set of the Western *MacKenna's Gold*.

Filmmaker 1968
Format 16mm. **Running time** 32 mins. With Francis Ford Coppola.
• A documentary chronicling the making of *The Rain People*, directed by Francis Ford Coppola.

FEATURE FILMS

THX 1138 1971
Screenplay George Lucas and Walter Murch. **Cinematography** Albert Kihn and David Myers. **Art Direction** Michael Haller **Editing** George Lucas and Marcia Lucas. **Music** Lalo Schifrin. **Production** American Zoetrope, Warner Brothers. **Distribution** Warner Brothers. **Running time** 1h 21 mins. With Robert Duvall (THX), Maggie McOmie (LUH), Donald Pleasence (SEN).
• In a twenty-fifth century totalitarian society, sex is outlawed and citizens are monitored and drugged into passive submission. Two roommates, THX (Duvall) and LUH (McOmie), stop taking their drugs and fall in love.

American Graffiti 1973
Screenplay George Lucas, Willard Huyck and Gloria Katz. **Cinematography** Jan D'Alquen, Ron Eveslage, and Haskell Wexler. **Editing** Verna Fields and Marcia Lucas. **Production** Francis Ford Coppola and Gary Kurtz. **Distribution** Universal Pictures. **Running time** 1h 48 mins. With Richard Dreyfuss (Curt), Ron Howard (Steve), Paul Le Mat (John), Charles Martin Smith (Terry the toad), Cindy Williams (Laurie), Candy Clark (Debbie), Mackenzie Phillips (Carol), Harrison Ford (Bob Falfa).
• Four teenage friends spend the final night of the summer of 1962 cruising around their small town, meeting girls and contemplating the future.

Star Wars 1977
Episode IV: A New Hope
Screenplay George Lucas. **Cinematography** Gilbert Taylor. **Production Design** John Barry. **Special Photographic Effects Supervisor** John Dykstra. **Editing** Richard Chew, Paul Hirsch, and Marcia Lucas. **Music** John Williams. **Production** Gary Kurtz. **Distribution** 20th Century Fox. **Running time** 2h 1 min. With Mark Hamill (Luke Skywalker), Harrison Ford (Han Solo), Carrie Fisher (Princess Leia Organa), David Prowse (Darth Vader), James Earl Jones (voice of Darth Vader), Peter Cushing (Grand Moff Tarkin), Alec Guinness (Obi-Wan Kenobi), Anthony Daniels (C-3PO), Kenny Baker (R2D2), Peter Mayhew (Chewbacca), Phil Brown (uncle Owen), Shelagh Fraser (aunt Beru), Alex McCrindle (General Dodonna), Eddie Byrne (General Willard), Don Henderson (General Taggi), Jack Purvis (Chief Jawa).
• A long time ago in a galaxy far, far away, the Rebel Alliance, led by Princess Leia (Fisher), is at war with the Empire, represented by Darth Vader, a vicious being half man and half machine. Luke Skywalker, a naïve country boy, and Han Solo, a roguish smuggler, are swept up into the Rebel cause.

Star Wars 1999
Episode I:
The Phantom Menace
Screenplay George Lucas. **Cinematography** David Tattersall. **Production Design** Gavin Bocquet. **Visual Effects Supervisor** John Knoll. **Editing** Ben Burtt and Paul Martin Smith. **Music** John Williams. **Production** Rick McCallum and George Lucas. **Distribution** 20th Century Fox. **Running time** 2h 13 mins. With Jake Lloyd (Anakin Skywalker), Liam Neeson (Qui-Gon Jinn), Ewan McGregor (Obi-Wan Kenobi), Natalie Portman (Queen Amidala / Padmé), Ian McDiarmid (Senator Palpatine), Anthony Daniels (voice of C-3PO), Kenny Baker (R2-D2), Frank Oz (voice of Yoda), Terence Stamp (Chancellor Valorum).
• Roughly thirty years before the events of *Star Wars*, Anakin Skywalker (Jake Lloyd) is a precocious slave boy whose connection to The Force raises the alarm of two Jedi knights, Qui-Gon Jinn (Liam Neeson) and Obi-Wan Kenobi (Ewan McGregor).

Star Wars 2002
Episode II:
Attack of the Clones
Screenplay George Lucas and Jonathan Hales. **Cinematography** David Tattersall. **Production Design** Gavin Bocquet. **Visual Effects Supervisor** John Knoll. **Editing** Ben Burtt. **Music** John Williams. **Production** Rick McCallum, George Lucas. **Distribution** 20th Century Fox. **Running time** 2 h 22 mins. With Hayden Christensen (Anakin Skywalker), Ewan McGregor (Obi-Wan Kenobi), Natalie Portman (Padmé), Ian McDiarmid (Supreme Chancellor Palpatine), Anthony Daniels (voice of C-3PO), Christopher Lee (Count Dooku / Darth Tyranus), Samuel L. Jackson (Mace Windu), Frank Oz (voice of Yoda), Temuera Morrison (Jango Fett), Daniel Logan (Boba Fett).
• Ten years after the events of *The Phantom Menace*, Anakin Skywalker (Christensen) is now studying the ways of the Force under Obi-Wan Kenobi. While Obi-Wan goes on a journey to investigate a threat to the Republic, Anakin is assigned to protect the beautiful senator, Padme Amidala (Portman). Padme and Anakin fall in love and secretly marry.

Star Wars 2005
Episode III:
Revenge of the Sith
Screenplay George Lucas. **Cinematography** David Tattersall. **Production Design** Gavin Bocquet. **Visual Effects Supervisor** John Knoll. **Editing** Roger Barton and Ben Burtt. **Music** John Williams. **Production** Rick McCallum and George Lucas. **Distribution** 20th Century Fox. **Running time** 2h 20 mins. With Hayden Christensen (Anakin Skywalker / Darth Vader), Ewan McGregor (Obi-Wan Kenobi), Natalie Portman (Padmé), Ian McDiarmid (Supreme Chancellor Palpatine / Darth Sidious), Christopher Lee (Count Dooku / Darth Tyranus), Samuel L. Jackson (Mace Windu), Frank Oz (voice of Yoda), Anthony Daniels (C-3PO).

• As he learns that Padme is pregnant with his baby, Anakin Skywalker finds his allegiance torn between, on the one hand, his mentor Obi-Wan Kenobi and the Jedi council and, on the other, Chancellor Palpatine (McDiarmid), who seduces Anakin toward the dark side of the Force by convincing him it's the only way to protect his wife and unborn child. At the end of the film, Anakin is transformed into the embodiment of evil, Darth Vader.

PRODUCER AND WRITER

Star Wars   **1980**
Episode V:
The Empire Strikes Back
by Irvin Kershner
Raiders of the Lost Ark 1981
by Steven Spielberg
Star Wars   **1983**
Episode VI:
Return of the Jedi
by Richard Marquand
Indiana Jones and   **1984**
the Temple of Doom
by Steven Spielberg
Captain EO   **1986**
by Francis Ford Coppola
Willow   **1988**
by Ron Howard
Indiana Jones and   **1989**
the Last Crusade
by Steven Spielberg
Radioland Murders   **1994**
by Mel Smith
Indiana Jones and   **2008**
the Kingdom of the
Crystal Skull
by Steven Spielberg

PRODUCER ONLY

More American   **1979**
Graffiti
by Bill L. Norton
Mishima: A Life   **1985**
in Four Chapters
by Paul Schrader
Labyrinth   **1986**
by Jim Henson
Howard the Duck   **1986**
by Willard Huyck
Powaqqatsi   **1988**
by Godfrey Reggio
Tucker: The Man   **1988**
and His Dream
by Francis Ford Coppola
Star Wars: **2008**
The Clone Wars
by Dave Filoni
Red Tails   **2012**
by Anthony Hemingway

Selected Bibliography

Sheerly Avni,
Cinema by the Bay.
New York: George Lucas, 2006.

Jennifer Bass and Pat Kirkham,
Saul Bass: A Life in Film & Design.
London: Laurence King, 2011.

John Baxter,
Mythmaker: The Life and Work of George Lucas.
New York: HarperCollins, 2000.

Peter Biskind,
Easy Riders, Raging Bulls: How the Sex 'n' Drugs 'n' Rock 'n' Roll Generation Changed Hollywood.
London: Bloomsbury, 1998.

Sally Kline (ed.),
George Lucas: Interviews.
Jackson: University Press of Mississippi, 1999.

J. W. Rinzler
and Laurent Bouzereau,
The Complete Making of Indiana Jones: The Definitive Story Behind All Four Films.
New York: Del Rey, 2008.

J. W. Rinzler
and Charles Lippincott,
The Making of Star Wars: The Definitive Story Behind the Original Film.
New York: Ballantine, 2007.

Michael Rubin,
Droidmaker: George Lucas and the Digital Revolution.
Gainesville, Florida: Triad Pub., 2006.

Kenneth VonGunden,
Postmodern Auteurs: Coppola, Lucas, De Palma, Spielberg, and Scorsese.
Jefferson, North Carolina: McFarland, 1991.

Notes

1. Silberman, Steve. "Life After Darth." *Wired*, May 2005.

2. Farber, Stephen. "George Lucas: The Stinky Kid Hits The Big Time." *Film Quarterly*, Spring 1974.

3. Biskind, Peter. *Easy Riders, Raging Bulls.* New York: Simon & Schuster, 1998, pp. 317–18.

4. Leva, Gary, dir. "A Legacy of Filmmakers: The Early Years of American Zoetrope." Warner Bros. Entertainment, 2004. Film.

5. Biskind, op. cit., p. 37.

6. Ibid.

7. Stone, Judy. "George Lucas." *San Francisco Chronicle*, May 23, 1971.

8. "THX 1138—Made in San Francisco." *American Cinematographer*, October 1971.

9. Ibid.

10. Ibid.

11. Biskind, op. cit., p. 98.

12. Ibid, p. 100.

13. Ibid, p. 92.

14. Vallely, Jean. "*The Empire Strikes Back* and So Does Filmmaker George Lucas With His Sequel to *Star Wars*," *Rolling Stone*, June 12, 1980.

15. Sturhahn, Larry. "The Filming of *American Graffiti*." *Filmmakers Newsletter*, March 1974.

16. Ibid.

17. Biskind, op. cit., p. 208.

18. Ibid, p. 143.

Notes

19. Rinzler, J. W. *The Making of Star Wars*, pp. 46–7.

20. Boucher, Geoff. "*Star Wars* producer Gary Kurtz speaks out." *Los Angeles Times*, August 12, 2010.

21. Pye, Michael and Linda Miles. *The Movie Brats*. Excerpted in *George Lucas: Interviews*, edited by Sally Kline.

22. Zito, Stephen. "George Lucas Goes Far Out." *American Film*, April 1977.

23. Ibid.

24. Rinzler, op. cit., p. 15.

25. Zito, op. cit.

26. Clouzot, Claire. "The Morning of the Magician: George Lucas and *Star Wars*." *Ercan*, Sept. 15, 1977.

27. Biskind, op. cit., p. 334.

28. Vallely, op. cit.

29. Zito, op. cit.

30. Baxter, John. *Mythmaker: The Life and Work of George Lucas*. Avon Books, 1999, p. 292.

31. Boucher, op. cit.

32. Kael, Pauline. *When the Lights Go Down*. New York: Holt, Rinehart and Winston, 1980, p. 291.

33. Harmetz, Aljean. "Burden of Dreams: George Lucas." *American Film*, June 1983.

34. Biskind, op. cit. p. 258.

35. Ebert, Roger. *Roger Ebert's Four Star Reviews 1967–2007*. Kansas City, Missouri: Andrews McMeel Publishing, 2007, p. 631.

36. Kael, Pauline. "The Current Cinema: Whipped." *The New Yorker*, June 15, 1981.

37. Baxter, op. cit., pp. 336–7.

38. McBride, Joseph. *Steven Spielberg: A Biography*. New York: Simon & Schuster, 1997, p. 355.

39. Cerone, Daniel. "ABC Gives 'Indiana' a Third Try: Harrison Ford to Guest on George Lucas's Ratings-Weak Show." *Los Angeles Times*, March 9, 1993.

40. Ebert, Roger. "*Willow*." *Chicago Sun-Times*, May 20, 1988.

41. King, Thomas, "Lucasvision." *Wall Street Journal*, March 1994.

42. Kline, Sally (ed.) *George Lucas: Interviews*. Jackson: University Press of Mississippi, 1999, p. 179.

43. Shone, Tom. *Blockbuster: How Hollywood learned to stop worrying and love the summer.* New York: Simon & Schuster, 2004, p. 218.

44. Kelly, Kevin and Paula Parisi. "Beyond Star Wars." *Wired*, February 1997.

45. Silberman, Steve. "George Lucas on *Star Wars*, *Fahrenheit 9/11*, and his own legacy." Wired.com, May 2005.

46. O'Quinn, Kerry. "The George Lucas Saga." *Starlog*, July–August–September, 1981.

47. Weiner, Rex. "Lucas the Loner Returns to *Wars*." *Weekly Variety*, June 5, 1995.

48. Hoberman, J. "All Droid Up." *Village Voice*, May 18, 1999.

49. Taylor, Charles. "The spirit is willing, but the Force is weak." Salon.com, May 19, 1999.

50. Maslin, Janet. "Film Review; In the Beginning, The Future." *New York Times*, May 19, 1999.

51. Silberman, op. cit.

52. Ebert, Roger. "*Star Wars Episode III: Revenge of the Sith*." *Chicago Sun-Times*, May 19, 2005.

53. Lane, Anthony. "The Current Cinema: Space Case." *The New Yorker*, May 23, 2005.
54. Franich, Darren. "New 'Return of the Jedi' Blu-ray has questionable addition: Darth Vader screaming 'Nooooo!'".

55. Sturhahn, op. cit.

56. Silberman, op. cit.

57. Faraci, Devin. "Lucas Added Vader Crying 'Noooooo!' To RETURN OF THE JEDI" *BadassDigest.com*, August 30, 2011.

58. Biskind, op. cit., p. 344.

59. Silberman, op. cit.

60. Ibid.